Discover ....

Idaho's Centennial Trail

Idaho
Centennial Trail

By Stephen Stuebner
and
The Idaho Trails Council

1

Copyright

Credits

Front cover photo: Roger Williams captures his hiking partner, Syd Tate, sizing up the view in the Spangle Lakes area of the Sawtooth Wilderness.
Back cover photos: The Bruneau Canyon, and inset of McGowan Peak in the Sawtooth Range. Photos by Roger Williams.
Cover design: Sally Stevens
Color photo-imaging: Michael Hewes Studio and Photography
Photo-scanning: Jeff Cook, Idaho Department of Parks and Recreation
Locator maps: Patrick Davis

Acknowledgments

The Idaho Trails Council would like to thank its long-time board member, officer and supporter, Roger Williams, for coming up with the vision for the Idaho State Centennial Trail. Several other Idaho Trails Council members, including Bernice Paige, Steve Gunderson, Lynn Brown, Chuck Wells and Leo Hennessy, have provided important leadership in establishing the trail route, ground-proofing portions of the trail, setting up a data base for trail conditions, and securing seed money for this guidebook. Thanks to all of the U.S. Forest Service staffers who reviewed the manuscript, and to the agency for its financial support. We also want to thank the Idaho Fish and Wildlife Foundation and the Nongame Watchable Wildlife program at Idaho Fish and Game for their financial support and assistance.

This guidebook has been a true collaborative effort. Roger Williams provided invaluable assistance in his knowledge of the Idaho backcountry. His fine photography is featured in most photos in the book. Special thanks to Jeff Cook for squeezing in time to scan photos for the book. Bernice Paige was very helpful in writing up the Sawtooth sections of the trail. Marty Morache also provided invaluable comments on the manuscript.

Finally, I'd like to thank my wife, Amy Stahl, for her proof-reading assistance, helpful comments and tolerance, considering this book was produced on weekends, evenings and early mornings in between taking care of our new son, Quinn Lewis Stuebner.

-- Stephen Stuebner

About the Idaho Trails Council ...

The Idaho Trails Council is a non-profit, statewide trail advocacy and educational group that seeks to represent all trail interests. It has been run by an all-volunteer board of directors for more than 25 years. The Idaho Trails Council was the chief proponent of creating a state trail in 1990 during the state's Centennial year. The Idaho State Centennial Trail is the result.

The Trails Council is governed by a 21-member board of directors, which includes positions for all trail groups and state and federal agencies. Trail interests on the board include paddle sports, urban trails, historic trails, hunters and anglers, snowmobiles, motorcycles, ATVs, llama packers, equestrians, hikers, cross-country skiers, and mountain bikes. Supporting agencies include the Idaho Department of Parks and Recreation, Idaho Department of Fish and Game, U.S. Forest Service, Bureau of Land Management, National Park Service, Idaho Department of Lands and Idaho Department of Transportation.

The Trails Council sponsors a trails symposium, held each year in a different part of Idaho, to discuss trail issues and take field trips to special trail projects or areas of trail conflict. The council plans to hold its 1998 symposium in McCall. The 1997 symposium was held in Wallace.

The Trails Council also puts out a newsletter six times a year. Memberships in the Trails Council cost $10 for individuals and $20 for agencies. Members receive free copies of the newsletter, and they receive the most comprehensive information on the fate of Idaho's trails on an ongoing basis.

Please consider joining the Trails Council and supporting Idaho's trails. If you'd like to join the Trails Council, send a check to the ITC, P.O. Box 1629, Sun Valley, ID 83353. Be sure to include your name, address, phone number and e-mail address.

For more information, call Bernice Paige, Trailhead editor, 208-622-3046. Her e-mail address is bepaige@micron.net.

Table of Contents

The Idaho State Centennial Trail
(South to North)

IDAHO STATE CENTENNIAL TRAIL

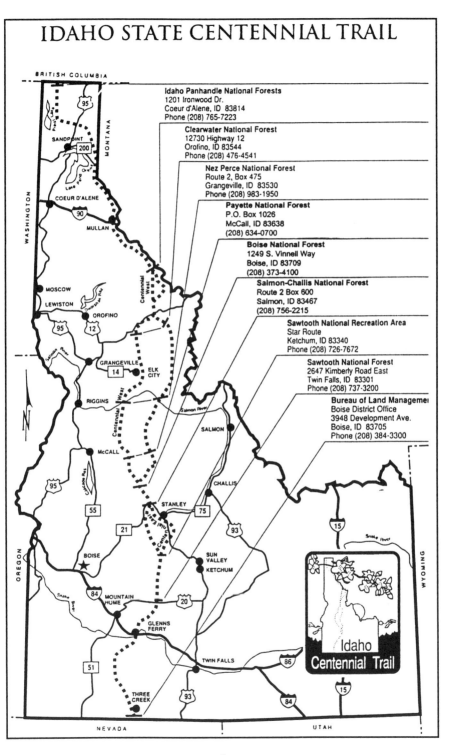

Idaho Panhandle National Forests
1201 Ironwood Dr.
Coeur d'Alene, ID 83814
Phone (208) 765-7223

Clearwater National Forest
12730 Highway 12
Orofino, ID 83544
Phone (208) 476-4541

Nez Perce National Forest
Route 2, Box 475
Grangeville, ID 83530
Phone (208) 983-1950

Payette National Forest
P.O. Box 1026
McCall, ID 83638
(208) 634-0700

Boise National Forest
1249 S. Vinnell Way
Boise, ID 83709
(208) 373-4100

Salmon-Challis National Forest
Route 2 Box 600
Salmon, ID 83467
(208) 756-2215

Sawtooth National Recreation Area
Star Route
Ketchum, ID 83340
Phone (208) 726-7672

Sawtooth National Forest
2647 Kimberly Road East
Twin Falls, ID 83301
Phone (208) 737-3200

Bureau of Land Managemer
Boise District Office
3948 Development Ave.
Boise, ID 83705
Phone (208) 384-3300

Idaho
Centennial Trail

WARNING

WARNING: BACKCOUNTRY TRAVEL INVOLVES A NUMBER OF UNAVOIDABLE RISKS THAT MAY CAUSE SERIOUS INJURY OR DEATH. THESE RISKS INCLUDE PHYSICAL INJURY, SEVERE WEATHER, MECHANICAL BREAKDOWNS AND GETTING LOST. ANYONE WHO PURCHASES THIS BOOK ASSUMES ALL RISK AND RESPONSIBILITY FOR THEIR OWN SAFETY AND WELFARE.

The authors have attempted to provide an accurate description of each section of the Idaho State Centennial Trail in this guidebook. However, a route listed in this book may or may not be safe for anyone to travel at any given time. Many of the routes are not signed, and the trail may be difficult to find. Routes vary in difficulty. Trails may change or deteriorate due to cataclysmic environmental or climatic events, logging, mining, road-building, wildfires, avalanches, mudslides, or other circumstances beyond the publishers' control.

We strongly urge trail users to check with the BLM or Forest Service before traveling any section of the Centennial Trail to determine the latest trail conditions.

The trail descriptions and other information in this book are designed to help people discover and follow the Idaho State Centennial Trail. We provide basic information about what to bring on the trail, how to prepare for your trip and who to contact for timely information. The time required to complete the trail sections will vary widely according to mode of travel and each person's level of endurance and ability.

Before you embark on a section of the Centennial Trail, tell someone where you are going and give them a map of the trail. If you get lost, search and rescue authorities recommend that you stay put, build a fire and wait for help. For search and rescue assistance, please call the emergency dispatch number for the county in which the person is lost.

Be honest with yourself. Know your limitations and use common sense.

Introduction

Welcome to the first-ever guidebook on the Idaho State Centennial Trail. A guide to the 1,200-mile Centennial Trail has been long overdue since the trail was officially established in 1990 during the state's Centennial year. But it has taken a number of years, with mostly volunteer effort, to ground-proof the route — a task that will be perpetual — post signs along the way, and gather as much historical and interpretive information about the trail as possible.

This book provides the best and only source of information printed to date on the detailed route, history and points of interest along the Centennial Trail. The route is extremely diverse — from old-growth cedar rainforest and grizzly bear habitat in the Upper Priest River to the clear, deep glaciated lakes in the Idaho Panhandle; from the jagged peaks of the Bitterroot Range along the Idaho-Montana state line to the lush forest and ferns of the Selway-Bitterroot Wilderness; from the heart of the Salmon River country in Chamberlain Basin to a walk along the Middle Fork of the Salmon River; from a tour through the core of the Sawtooth Wilderness, whose spectacular spire-studded peaks are the most scenic in the state, to a parallel hike alongside the yawning Bruneau and Jarbidge river canyons in southwest Idaho.

The Centennial Trail offers a glimpse of sagebrush-steppe habitat indicative of the Great Basin, alpine mountain ecosystems in central Idaho, and wet mountain terrain that's analogous to coastal rainforests in the Panhandle. The trail touches many points of historical interest, too — it crosses the Oregon Trail, the Nez Perce Trail, and the Lewis and Clark Trail. It passes through many old mining districts and old homesteads in the Salmon River country. The geology of the trail is diverse, too, giving visitors a sense of how basalt and rhyolite lava flows, the Idaho Batholith, ancient lakes, glaciation and other geologic events that have formed the state's unique landscape.

People may not choose to travel the entire length of the Centennial Trail in one summer, as pioneers Roger Williams and Syd Tate did in 1986, but once they become familiar with the route, it's something that can be done in segments, one trip at a time. For some folks, it may become a lifelong goal to travel the length of the trail.

Unlike most other long-distance trails, such as the Pacific Crest Trail, the Idaho Centennial Trail is open to more than just hikers and equestrians. The trail is a mixture of single-track trails, jeep trails and dirt roads. About one-third of the route is open to multiple use, meaning trail bikes, mountain bikes, ATVs, snowmobiles and motor vehicles. In cases where the Centennial Trail cuts through wilderness areas, where no motor vehicles are allowed, special alternative routes have been established to provide passage for motorized trail use and mountain bikes.

Before you venture out on the Centennial Trail, please read through the chapter on special equipment and information you might need on the trail. After you complete a section of the Centennial Trail, please fill out and send in the form in the back of the book on trail conditions. Help the Idaho Trails Council stay current on trail conditions, obstacles or other helpful information. Because the trail covers so many miles of remote backcountry, the Trails Council needs to hear from people

A sunny day on Patrol Ridge, above Running Creek, near the Selway-Bitterroot Wilderness in north-central Idaho.

who actually visit the trail at ground-level to provide the best information to the public on a continuing basis.

A word of caution on the maps that we provide in the book. The maps illustrate the "big picture" view of the 23 segments of the Centennial Trail, but they should not be used for navigation. The Idaho Trails Council strongly recommends that anyone who travels the Centennial Trail should purchase a general forest map or BLM map of the route they're traveling, highlight the route on a large-scale map, and then pick up detailed U.S. Geological Survey 7.5-minute topographical maps of the trail route for the best guidance in the field. Each trail segment in the guide tells you the name of the "topo" maps you'll need.

Enjoy!

Roger Williams

Black bears frequent all of the national forests in Idaho.

The Idaho Centennial Trail

Lasting Legacy Committee designates trail in 1990

In 1986, two Idaho men, Roger Williams and Syd Tate, trekked the length of Idaho through the most remote backcountry possible. Their south-to-north, 1,200-mile crossing of Idaho created the vision for the Idaho Centennial Trail.

Williams, a longtime member and past president of the Idaho Trails Council, a statewide trail-advocacy group, pitched the notion of an official north-south trail through Idaho at the annual meeting of the Idaho Trails Council in the spring of 1987. He gave a slide show on his odyssey through Idaho's incredibly rugged and diverse landscape, and sold the Trails Council on the idea. Although the notion of a statewide trail had been advanced casually before, no one had ever selected an actual route. The trails selected by Williams and Tate in their 1986 trip became the starting point for discussions on an official route.

Williams and other officers of the Idaho Trails Council began pushing the idea in political circles and among all the key natural resources agencies to get the ball rolling. In 1989, the idea gained more momentum when Williams was named to sit on the Lasting Legacy Committee, a panel that would select special historic projects as part of the Idaho Centennial celebration in 1990, the anniversary of Idaho's statehood. Williams sold the Lasting Legacy Committee on the concept with his color slide show, and the Centennial Commission officially adopted the project as a way to showcase Idaho's outstanding scenic beauty, colorful history and culture. The Idaho Parks & Recreation Board and department staff were very supportive of the project and helped move it along.

A Centennial Trail agency steering committee and citizens advisory committee were formed to select an official route. It was a difficult struggle to find a route agreeable to all trail user groups and environmental groups, eight different national forests and several different Bureau of Land Management districts. A special facilitator mediated the meetings. The trail-selection process called "Choosing by Advantage," in bureaucratic parlance, was used to narrow down the route.

Williams' and Tate's route was retained in some instances and rejected in others. Alternative routes called Centennial West and Centennial East were designated to provide north-south corridors for trail uses banned in wilderness areas to run parallel with the Sawtooth Wilderness, the Frank Church-River of No Return Wilderness, the Selway-Bitterroot Wilderness and Gospel-Hump Wilderness.

After many months of meetings and emotional anguish, a final route was adopted by the Idaho Parks & Recreation Board and all participating national forests and BLM districts. As it turned out, the painful debates paid off: the Centennial Trail takes visitors on a tour of Idaho's finest landscapes.

The Pioneers —
Roger Williams and Syd Tate

An 86-day sojourn through rugged Idaho creates the vision
for the 1,200-mile Idaho Centennial Trail

The first golden ray of sunlight bounced off shiny columns of basalt in Black Rock Canyon, deep in the Owyhee desert on the Idaho-Nevada border. Syd Tate was up with the sun, getting the campfire going for breakfast. As the fire began to crackle, Tate stared at the flames. He had a slight knot in his gut that morning, an extra dose of adrenaline in anticipation of the monumental journey ahead. He

looked up at the sky, and at the soft yellow light forming on the basalt canyon wall. He knew, somehow, that he and hiking partner, Roger Williams, were going to make it. After five years of preparation, they finally were about to begin the south-to-north backcountry trek through Idaho. By Williams' plan, they would average 14 miles a day, for 86 days, to hike 1,200 miles through one of the most rugged states in the nation.

Roger Williams

Syd Tate and Roger Williams begin their journey in June 1986 on the Idaho-Nevada border. Friend John Beecham, middle, hiked the first leg with the duo.

Here at the Idaho-Nevada border, Tate, the owner of Tates Rents, an Idaho home-grown chain of rental-equipment stores, and Williams, a retired wildlife biologist for the Idaho Fish and Game Department, would begin the journey under blazing hot, clear days on the Owyhee Plateau, at an elevation of 5,900 feet.

They would start along the west side of the West Fork of the Bruneau River, a deep chasm with rare access. The canyon is rimmed by rhyolite and basalt lava rock, a magnificent display of spires, columns, vertical walls, rapids and waterfalls. It's a gorgeous view, walking along the rim of the canyon, and it's so remote that it's easy to feel alone, quite insignificant in the whole scheme of things. In the uplands of the Owyhee Plateau, endless slopes of sagebrush and juniper roll on for infinity. No roads, powerlines or development. Just you, the canyon, the sagebrush and the howl of coyotes.

That was how Williams and Tate wanted it. Williams selected a route that traced through the wildest, most remote and least developed parts of Idaho. They could have started the hike in May, but they didn't want to run into snow and high water in the Sawtooth Mountains, some 4,000 feet higher, to the north. Once they hit the Sawtooths, they would be hiking through the gnarly interior of Idaho — the Salmon River Mountains, the Selway Bitterroot Wilderness, the craggy Idaho-Montana divide above the St. Joe River, and onward into the wettest region of Idaho, the white pine and cedar forests of the Panhandle. Waiting for the snow to clear made sense.

But by June 21, the days were sizzling hot in the Owyhee desert. "We hiked in the mornings and evenings and shaded up in the middle of the day," Tate recalls, grinning at the challenge. This backpacking duo had a ton of experience. They possessed a strong can-do type of attitude. A little heat wasn't going to set them back. They were on their way.

"At no time did I entertain the thought that we weren't going to make it," Tate says. "We *were* going to make it. It was a given."

It seems appropriate that Williams, 59, and Tate, 52, tackled the pioneering effort to make a south-to-north crossing of Idaho in the most remote terrain possible. These guys started backpacking well before it was the vogue thing to do. Williams, a longtime big game hunter, says his first backpack trip was in 1958 on a mountain goat hunting trip. He had built his own pack frame, using a detailed pattern from the book, *On Your Own in the Wilderness,* by Col. Townsend Whelen. He'd wrap his grub, cook kit, clothes and rain gear in canvas and plastic, and lash it to the pack frame. The backpack didn't have a waist belt, and the shoulder straps didn't have any foam padding. Tate started out with the same gear as a Boy Scout.

Tate and Williams met each other as adults in church. Their families lived in the same part of town, so they used to car-pool their kids to Sunday school, and they got together for social occasions. The bond grew tighter as Roger and Syd sang in a barbershop quartet together (Roger sang bass; Syd tenor). Roger's wife, Elinor, and Sid's wife, Mary, enjoyed each other's company, and they both liked the outdoors, too. Pretty soon the families began to go camping together. Since they both enjoyed camping and hiking in the mountains, Syd and Roger started to take their kids backpacking as soon as the kids were old enough to carry some of their own gear. "The kids were the incentive to go out and pack together," Tate says. This was in the early 1960s.

Both men raised their children, built successful careers and continued to venture into the mountains on a regular basis through the 1970s. In the early 1980s, Roger raised the idea of doing the first-known east-west hike through Idaho, on a route that avoided roads, towns and development to the maximum extent. "I mentioned the idea to Syd, and he said, `Let's go!' " Williams says. "That was just like Syd. He was always game for adventure."

The twosome agreed to tackle the 250-mile hike in the summer of 1981. They would complete the trek in three weeks. They took a jet boat down the Snake River in Hells Canyon — the nation's deepest gorge — to a point near the mouth of

Granite Creek and began the hike. The route took them through some of the most vertical up-and-down terrain anywhere. They started at an elevation of 1,400-feet at the edge of the Snake River in Hells Canyon, and their route climbed to points above 8,000 feet, before dropping into the next valley. They arranged for three food drops along the way -- at Rapid River, Burgdorf Hot Springs and the Salmon River, near Lantz Bar.

Roger Williams

Taking a moment to soak in the view at Elk Lake in the heart of the Sawtooth Mountains.

It was a fun and rewarding trip, Williams recalls. "Toward the end, we thought, hey, we're having so much fun, why don't we try something else? Once we had hiked across the state, what's the next logical thing to do?"

Williams tilts his head, and his blue eyes sparkle. They would have to hike the *length* of Idaho. As a career-long wildlife biologist, Williams had poked around most of the wilderness and back-country areas of Idaho.

He knew how tough it was to hike across the desert — the heat makes your throat dry and the rough rocky terrain rips away at your feet. He knew how tough it was to climb over countless mountain passes into alpine lakes basins. He knew they'd get drenched in the rain. But to people like Williams and Tate, guys who love to be in the outdoors, guys who have a constant itch to see "new country" and enjoy big vista-views, the notion of hiking the length of Idaho is an ultimate lifetime adventure.

Due to his wide travels through the backcountry of Idaho, and his skill with a map, Williams was the architect of the route through Idaho. "It took me five years, off and on, to put the route together," Williams says. "The main thing was to avoid roads and developments, and given a choice, stay high."

He also wanted to walk through the "best of Idaho" in places such as the Bruneau Canyon, the Sawtooth Wilderness, the Middle Fork of the Salmon, Chamberlain Basin, the Selway Bitterroot Wilderness, the high divide on the Idaho-Montana border, and the Panhandle lakes. Starting from the Nevada border, the backpacking duo would drop 3,400 feet in elevation to the Snake River, and then climb to the route's high point of 9,500 feet above Redfish Lake in the Sawtooths. Then, the route would take them on a roller-coaster ride through the mountain interior of Idaho for hundreds of miles. The lowest point of the route was 1,700 feet near the Kootenai River at the Canadian border.

Their ever-so-generous wives, and Syd's parents, would resupply them with food 12 times (about once a week). They completed the journey on Sept. 14 at the Canadian border.

"We made it without serious mishap," Williams says. "And we had one tremendous, once-in-a-lifetime experience."

Tate enjoyed the mellow feeling he got on the summer-long trek, just taking it one step at a time, one day at a time. "You just get into a mindset that doesn't really compare with anything else," he says. "If you're out for a three-day trip, you get a mindset for a three-day trip. When you're out for almost three months, you don't really think about anything more than what you've got in front of you on that particular day. Every day was different. We always looked forward to the next day and what it would bring."

Williams' route — that is, often staying high on ridges for the best views — allowed them to look back and see where they'd been the day before, and to see the landscape unfolding ahead.

Roger Williams

A rainy night in the Idaho Panhandle.

"Some of the ridges were so high we could look back and see where we'd been even two days before," Tate says.

Both men used external frame packs for the journey. They started out with a cook stove, a water purifier and a small wood saw, but when they got into the woods on Soldier Mountain, they ditched all of that equipment to save on weight. For the rest of the trip, they cooked all of their meals in their trail-worn pots and pans on a stick fire. They each carried four quarts of water. "The farther along we went, we realized that we could get by with less and less and less," Tate says. "The nice thing about backpacking is it's about the most simple way to enjoy life as there is. The key is to keep it simple. We jettisoned things as we went along."

In the last third of the hike, they ran into rainy weather — for five days in a row. Finding dry wood was a challenge, Tate recalls, but keeping their sleeping bags and clothes dry after that many consecutive days of rain was really difficult. "It was tough," he recalls. Williams had arranged to stay in a fish hatchery on the fifth night, near the town of Clark Fork. Both of them were greatly relieved to get out of the rain for a night and dry out their things. Tate remembers that they looked quite ragged.

"We were skin and bones," Tate says. "I had a beard sticking way out, and Roger was looking pretty scruffy, too." Fish hatchery personnel "were pretty wary of these odd-balls who showed up at their door."

Both men invited family members and close friends to join them on the hike. Fish and Game wildlife research supervisor John Beecham joined them for the first leg of the hike in the desert, and rejoined them at the trip's conclusion near the Canadian border. Tate's daughter, Paula, and her husband, Adam, hiked with them from the Salmon River, near Corn Creek, to the Magruder Road on the edge of the Selway Bitterrroot Wilderness. His son, Eric, joined them at Hoodoo Pass for a rugged trek along the spine of the Idaho-Montana border, known as the Stateline trail. And Syd's youngest son, Clint, walked with them down the Middle Fork of the Salmon River. Williams' nephew from Pennsylvania, Dave McCandless, joined them for a walk down the Selway River from Paradise to Moose Creek and then over to the Lochsa River near Powell.

> "I can't think of anything better than spending an enjoyable summer hiking the Centennial Trail. Idaho is such a diverse state, and you never fully appreciate that until you've hiked the length of the state, from the desert, to the mountains, to the rivers, to the rainforest. It's quite a place."
>
> -- *Syd Tate*

On any trip of this kind, there were high points and low points. One of Williams' favorite moments was when they stood on the shoulder of 7,930-foot Rhodes Peak, overlooking the headwaters of Kelly Creek, a pristine blue-ribbon fishing stream in the Clearwater National Forest. "I had seen the Sawtooths before, and I had been down the Middle Fork, but that Kelly Creek country was really neat," he says. "It's different country. It's big, remote and impressive. From where we stood, we could see all three big tributaries of Kelly Creek going up against the divide, and we could see several high lakes in the headwaters. It was a pretty neat spot."

Tate remembers the segment of the trail from the Lochsa to the Stateline trail as being among his most favorite moments, too. "Up on top of the border trail, I never felt further away from the rest of the world," he says. "We saw an Idaho-Montana marker, and I felt, boy, we are by ourselves up here. It's quite rocky and there's a lot of exposed granite. From the Idaho side, the terrain fell away kind of gently, but on the Montana side, there were sheer drops into many high lake basins. There was a new lakes basin around almost every bend."

Both men remember the section north of Hoodoo Pass as being among the most difficult segments of the hike. Williams' route kept them on some dry ridgelines that tested their water capacity of two gallons a day. "The most memorable tough day to me was from Moose Creek Ranger Station (near the Selway River) to Bailey Mountain," Tate says. "We climbed up a south slope that was very hot. We got to a point where we had used all of our water supply, and we finally found a seep of water near the top."

Williams recalls the heat as being the toughest part of the trip, along the Bruneau in June, and along the Stateline trail in August. "We were really thrashing through a lot of brush on dry south slopes," he says. "That was pretty tough."

At times, they had to drop from ridgetops and bushwack for water. Some nights they'd go dry and hope to run into water on the next day's hike. "There were times when we got thirsty at night," Tate says. "A gallon of water could get pretty thin." On one

Roger Williams

A familiar sight in Chamberlain Basin in the Frank Church Wilderness, a pack string of mules and horses.

night north of Lookout Pass, for instance, Williams recalls that they were very short on water, after a long, dry day, even though they had just been resupplied. "So we sorted through all the freeze-dried dinners to find the one that required the least water (for cooking)." They picked a spicy Mexican dish. "After dinner we second-guessed that decision," Williams says.

The hiking duo ran into some tough luck in Clark Fork, the only town along the route, where they arrived on Labor Day weekend. They had been short a day's rations from the previous resupply, so they hiked into town a day early. Counting on a Visa credit card to buy a meal in a restaurant, they were chagrined to learn that no one took Visa in town. So they scraped together a few bucks for a lean meal. They had to settle for a candy bar lunch on their "shopping day" in Clark Fork. "We left town with 12 cents between us -- including the dime I found on the street!" Williams recalls. "Good thing Elinor stuck a $20 bill in the resupply box she sent us."

North Idaho presented several difficulties, such as dense fog. It was the closest they ever came to getting lost. But along with the guidance of a compass, they followed an old wilderness phone line that kept them on track. "We were glad

15

it was there," Tate says.

On Sept. 14, Williams and Tate hiked the last leg of the journey down Long Canyon and along the west side of Kootenai River road to Boundary Creek — aptly named, of course — and, 100 yards north, crossed into Canada in the rainforest. They had done it.

Their wives joined them for a champagne toast at the border, and they drove back to Coeur d'Alene to clean up and devour a tasty first-class meal. "My wife met me with a razor," Tate says, grinning. He'd been wearing a beard for five years, but now he — and she — was ready to get rid of the fuzz.

At the trip's conclusion, the two scruffy guys looked each other over and realized that their bodies had been transformed. Both of the athletic men had lost about 20 pounds. "Our legs looked like a weight lifter's and the top half looked like a prisoner of war," Williams said.

Over nearly 90 days in the Idaho backcountry, Williams and Tate had seen

They made it! Syd and Roger are a couple of happy fellas at the Canadian border, after covering 1,200 miles in 86 days in the summer of 1986.

Roger Williams

only a dozen people on the trail. They saw most people rafting down the Middle Fork. They enjoyed many views of wildlife, but not quite as many as they had hoped. They saw a few coyotes, elk, deer, antelope, bighorn sheep, black bear, one marten, 110 species of birds and "a good number of rattlesnakes." They didn't run into a mountain goat, and they never saw a grizzly.

Best of all, though, they had stuck together as friends, they didn't get lost, and neither one of them sustained a major injury.

"There's an extreme amount of satisfaction that comes with a trip like that," Tate says. "I can't think of anything better than spending an enjoyable summer hiking the Centennial Trail. Idaho is such a diverse state, and you never fully appreciate that until you've hiked the length of the state, from the desert, to the mountains, to the rivers, to the rainforest. It's quite a place."

Before you go ...
Essential gear and information

There are many things to think about and consider before packing up for a major backcountry adventure in the wild outback of Idaho. Here are a few basic things to remember:

Water: Carry lots of water, and bring a good-quality water purifier to replenish supplies. Top off your water bottles at every opportunity.

Rain gear: Be sure to carry a good-quality raincoat, rain pants, and some kind of rain cover for your packs.

Hat: A broad-brimmed hat provides protection from the sun, heat and rain. Sunglasses, sun screen and lip protection are recommended, too.

First-Aid kit: A well-stocked first-aid kit should be part of your required gear. Many outdoor stores sell kits of varying sizes and supplies, for your vehicle and for carrying on the trail.

Bug stuff: Make sure you always carry potent bug juice to keep the mosquitoes, gnats and biting flies out of your face.

Map and compass: Each trail description lists the general maps and detailed topographical maps you'll need for each segment of the Centennial Trail.

Tell someone where you're going, and when you're coming back.

Call ahead to check on the latest conditions: It's always a good idea to contact the BLM or the U.S. Forest Service to check on trail conditions. Windstorms, floods, mudflows and other natural events can wreak havoc on the trail, and local recreation staffers are usually aware of whether such events have caused problems in particular areas. From BLM lands in southern Idaho, to national forests heading north, here are the contact numbers to reach recreation officers:

1. Bureau of Land Management, Jarbidge Resource Area, 208-736-2358; Bruneau Resource Area, 208-384-3300.
2. Sawtooth National Forest, Fairfield Ranger District, 208-764-2202.
3. Sawtooth National Recreation Area, 208-726-7672.
4. Stanley Ranger District, 208-774-3681.
5. Salmon-Challis National Forests, Middle Fork District, 208-879-4101.
6. Boise National Forest, Cascade District, 208-382-4271.
7. Payette National Forest, McCall, 208-634-0700.
8. Nez Perce National Forest, Grangeville, 208-983-1950.
9. Clearwater National Forest, Orofino, 208-476-4541; Kelly Forks, 476-5877.
10. Idaho Panhandle National Forests:
     -- St. Joe National Forest, Avery, 208-245-4517.
     -- Coeur d'Alene National Forest, Wallace area, 208-752-1221.
     -- Sandpoint Ranger District, 208-263-5111.
     -- Bonners Ferry Ranger District, 208-267-5561.
12. Idaho Dept. of Lands, Sandpoint, 208-263-5104.
13. Idaho Dept. of Parks & Recreation, headquarters, 208-334-4199.

Backcountry ethics
Practice common courtesy & minimum impact

BASIC GUIDELINES FOR ALL TRAIL USERS

♦ Stay on trails and don't cut switchbacks, take shortcuts or create new trails.

♦ Be considerate of fellow trail users.

♦ Wheeled vehicle users should avoid harsh maneuvers that damage trail tread.

♦ Avoid muddy trails. Save them for future trips when they are dry.

♦ Keep your party small, preferably less than five. Littering is unacceptable. Set an example and pick up after others.

♦ Never leave fishing gear and litter in or along waterways. It can kill wildlife. Do not leave fish remains in lakes and streams.

♦ Remove obstacles from trails when possible.

♦ Avoid deliberately disturbing wildlife, especially in winters and during calving and fawning. Observe from a distance.

♦ Ride or walk on the center of trail tread to protect uphill slope and outside berm.

♦ Place gates to be closed perpendicular to the fence line. Those to be left open should be parallel to the fence line.

♦ Do not disturb archaeological or historic sites, or natural features.

Idaho Wildlife

Centennial Trail travelers should watch for a wide variety of birds and wildlife

From the cool, moist forests of the Panhandle to the hot sagebrush plains of the Snake and Bruneau rivers, Idaho's diverse landscape is home to an equally diverse group of wildlife. In their book *Mammals of Idaho*, Earl Larrison and Donald Johnson write, ". . .the state of Idaho 'borrows' faunas and floras from neighboring physiographic provinces. A taste of the North country may be found in the caribou and bog lemming of the northern Pan-handle. The mountain goat and elk remind us that the Bitterroot and Salmon River Mountains are a part of the Northern Rockies. The Columbian ground squirrel relates the

Gary Will

A side-blotched lizard poses on a rock in the Owyhee Desert.

Palouse country to the Columbia River Plateau, while the strong influence of the Great Basin may be felt in the desert regions of Southern Idaho with such species as the antelope squirrel, kangaroo rats, and pocket mice."

For a variety of reasons, including questions on historical records for some species and the accidental visitations by many bird species to the state, the exact number of vertebrate species will never be known. The best estimate of wildlife officials is that there are 589 species, including 83 fishes, 15 amphibians, 23 reptiles, 360 birds, and 108 mammals that occur in Idaho. Up to 10 percent of these species are introduced or non-native, the majority of which are fish. Also, you can rest assured that you'll be accompanied by insects and other invertebrates during your entire trek! To understand the range and distribution of Idaho's birds, refer to field guides, regional checklists and the databases of the Conservation Data Center of the Idaho Department of Fish and Game. These and other publications and leaflets about Idaho's wildlife are available at bookstores and from state and federal agencies.

Idaho Wildlife

Otters frequent most of Idaho's rivers and lakes. They're curious critters: they often pop up out of the water and check out humans who pass through their territory.

IDFG

Approximate number of vertebrate species occurring in Idaho:

	Fish	Amphibians	Reptiles	Birds	Mammals	Total
Species	83	15	23	360	108	589
Introduced species	41	1	0	12	6	60
Game species	38	1	0	48	24	111
Nongame species	45	14	23	309	77	468
Protected nongame spec.	4	3	0	309	11	327
Endemic species	6	0	0	0	1	7

Outdoor enthusiasts who journey along parts or all of the Centennial Trail are likely to encounter a variety of critters. The greatest variety of reptiles will be found in the deserts of southern Idaho, where the trail begins at the Nevada border. Many of the 23 species of reptiles may be encountered here, including (keep your eyes and ears open) the rattlesnake. Be especially alert for a host of other species in riparian areas—that strip of vegetation associated with streams. In the desert, a riparian area acts as an oasis for

Marty Morache

Pikas, the smallest members of the rabbit family, signal their presence in mountain talus slopes with a high-pitched "eek!"

20

Idaho Wildlife

wildlife. Where there's water and associated riparian vegetation, there is bound to be a variety of birds, mammals, reptiles and an occasional amphibian. Look for owls, lazuli buntings, northern orioles and yellow-breasted chats in riparian areas. Watch for ravens, golden eagles, turkey vultures, prairie falcons, ferruginous hawks, red-tailed hawks and Swainson's hawks flying overhead in the open desert. On the sagebrush plateau, you may see jackrabbits, cottontail rabbits, Townsend's ground squirrels, coyotes, badgers and the ever-present magpie throughout the desert trek. The secretive bobcat patrols the canyon rims.

Gary Will

Idaho has the second largest population of Rocky Mountain elk in the United States, next to Colorado.

No matter what part of the trail you're on, you're bound to be greeted by a squirrel, chipmunk or some other rodent. Chipmunks and golden-mantled ground squirrels can often be found begging for handouts along the trail or in camp. The noisy ever-present red squirrel will surely escort you through pine and spruce-covered forests. While they may be seen throughout

Craig Groves

Harlequin ducks are found on fast-moving streams like the Lochsa and Selway rivers.

Idaho's forests, don't expect to see a northern flying squirrel, unless you're noctur-nal like them.

Leaving the desert and ascending into the diverse forests along the Centennial Trail will expose travelers to an even wider variety of common and not-so-common wildlife. Idaho's forests, streams, meadows and mountain tops will serve up many

Idaho Wildlife

Wayne Melquist

It's always a treat to see a family of mountain goats.

IDFG

The marten is a shy forest carnivore, like the wolverine and fisher. Very little is known about the range and habits of marten because they're so secretive and difficult to study.

chance sightings for all wildlife watchers. The drier old-growth ponderosa pine forests are home to the Lewis' woodpecker—the only woodpecker that forages for insects on the wing—the pileated woodpecker, and others of the woodpecking variety. The more moist montane forests of higher elevations are home to the gray jay (often referred to as the "camp robber"). Sooner or later you're bound to be visited by these delightful birds, in camp, or along the trail, especially if you leave food out. Watch for the brilliant blue Steller's jay as you • travel the forests and the Clark's nutcracker in coniferous forests near timberline.

Idaho's forests are also home to a host of forest carnivores, most of which you're unlikely to get a glimpse of. Marten, fisher, and wolverine, all members of the weasel

Idaho Wildlife

family, inhabitat the coniferous forests of central and northern Idaho. A glimpse of one of these creatures would surely be a rewarding experience. You may see spawning salmon, otters or mink as you travel along the larger rivers and tributaries. Don't forget to keep your eyes open, and ears tuned, for the dipper or water ouzel—a small, dark bird that "walks under water" in search of aquatic insects. These birds nest and raise their young along Idaho's clear, pristine mountain streams.

Wayne Melquist

Rocky Mountain bighorn sheep are commonly seen on the steep cliffs of the Salmon River canyon.

Mountain meadows, lakes and forest edges are good places to look for Idaho's state bird—the mountain bluebird, or a moose. Keep your distance from moose, however, because a moose with a calf can be a very dangerous animal! If you miss the opportunity to see one of Idaho's wolves, listen for their lonely howl, which is much deeper and mournful than the "yapping" coyote. High elevation forest edges are good places to listen for the olive-sided flycatcher singing its "quick, three beers" song from high atop a large fir tree.

Talus hillsides and rocky areas are good places to spot mountain goats, pikas (rock rabbits) and marmots. Pikas build their nests and store hay in the boulders.

Meadows, old burns, and huckleberry hillsides in the Selkirk Mountains of north Idaho are the domain of grizzly bears. Hughes Meadows has long been known for grizzlies in spring. In winter, when grizzlies sleep, woodland caribou can be found on high ridges, feeding on arboreal lichens 10-30 feet above the ground. The deep winter snows make this food source accessible to the caribou, commonly referred to as "bigfoot of the north" because their large hooves allow them to walk through deep snow.

Watch for ospreys diving for fish or perching from their nests atop of snags and tall pine trees when you reach Lake Pend Oreille and Priest Lake.

The Idaho Trails Council would like to develop a checklist of birds and other wildlife found along the Centennial Trail. Have fun building a list of species observed as you journey across Idaho, and share it with us. Please compile a list of species observed with the following information: location of trail where they were seen, date and time, general habitat, and any other pertinent information you feel would be beneficial. Send your information to the Nongame and Watchable Wildlife Program, Idaho Department of Fish and Game, P.O. Box 25, Boise, ID 83707. Happy wildlife watching! -- *By Wayne Melquist, with Marty Morache*

23

Idaho Wilderness

The Idaho State Centennial Trail winds through a portion of three federally designated wilderness areas, and skirts a fourth. That's because Roger Williams wanted the 1,200-mile route to pass through the most remote and beautiful parts of Idaho. All of these wilderness areas have national significance in terms of their beauty and outstanding natural values. Here are a few notes about the genesis of each wilderness area, and what you can expect to find there.

The Sawtooth Wilderness: In 1972, the 216,000-acre Sawtooth Wilderness was protected by Congress, with the late Sen. Frank Church, D-Idaho, and Democratic Gov. Cecil Andrus leading the charge. The Sawtooth is the most heavily used wilderness area in Idaho, with more than 33,000 visitors per year. The Centennial Trail cuts through the central core of the Sawtooth range, providing awe-inspiring views of its many needle-like peaks. The pink granite rock in the Sawtooths is a major draw for rock climbers in certain areas. The wilderness is chock-full of emerald-like high mountain lakes, alpine meadows and choice campsites.

The Frank Church-River of No Return Wilderness: Congress created the largest single wilderness in the lower 48 states when it set aside 2.4 million acres of central Idaho as the Frank Church-River of No Return Wilderness in 1980. It was a hotly contested political fight to determine how much of the Central Idaho Primitive Area would be official wilderness. Once again, Sen. Church showed the political courage to lead the way to protect nearly all of the Middle Fork Salmon River corridor, and about 80 miles of the main Salmon River. To stand on top of a peak in the heart of "the Frank" is a breathtaking experience, knowing that the seemingly endless sea of mountains unfolding before your eyes is wilderness as far as you can see in all directions. There are an estimated 850 high mountain lakes in "the Frank" as well as many tributaries of the Salmon River, the spectacular Big Horn Crags, the extensive meadow complex in Chamberlain Basin, and so much more.

The Selway-Bitterroot Wilderness: The 1.28-million-acre Selway-Bitterroot Wilderness was considered to be so deserving of protection that it was among the first group of so-called "instant" wilderness areas set aside by Congress when it passed the Wilderness Act in 1964. The late Sen. Frank Church, D-Idaho, was one of the chief architects of the act. The Selway-Bitterroot features densely forested mountains, the Selway Crags, many mountain meadows, lots of high mountain lakes, and the wild and scenic Selway River, a pristine gin-clear stream that's full of rapids and cutthroat trout. It's very likely that you'll encounter elk and moose in this area.

The Gospel Hump Wilderness: Portions of the Centennial West route from the Wind River Pack Bridge on the Salmon River to Selway Falls wrap around the western and northern boundary of the 206,000-acre Gospel-Hump Wilderness in the Nez Perce National Forest. The Gospel Hump was protected by Congress in 1978, with the late Sen. Frank Church, D-Idaho, leading the way. The Gospel Hump features a number of high mountain lakes, deep and broad valleys and lush meadows.

The Guide

Roger Williams

A group of hikers cross over Hansen Ridge, north of Kelly Creek.

Let the journey begin ....

#1 ID-Nev. line to Clover-Three Cr. Rd.

South access: Murphy Hot Springs
North access: Clover-Three Creek Road,
near Bruneau Canyon overlook
Distance: 87 miles
High point: Idaho-Nevada state line, 5,991
Low point: Clover-Three Creek Road jct.,
3,500 feet
Type of trail: Primitive 4WD jeep trail
Uses allowed: Hiking, horseback, mountain
bikes, motorcycles, ATVs, 4WD vehicles
Terrain: High desert plateau, undulating
rough and rocky terrain
Season: May to late October
Access to water: Spotty; be sure to carry
plenty

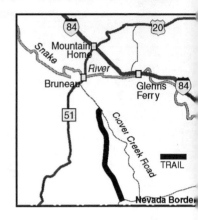

Overview map: Murphy Hot Springs, BLM map
Topo maps: Murphy Hot Springs, Dishpan, Poison Butte, The Arch, Inside Lakes, Stiff Tree Draw, Winter Camp, Crowbar Gulch, Hot Spring.

Directions to South Access: To reach Murphy Hot Springs, you can either drive to Bruneau via Idaho 51 from Mountain Home and take the Clover-Three Creek Road, a single-lane gravel road, about 65 miles to Murphy Hot Springs. Or, you can drive to Twin Falls, head south to Rogerson on U.S. 93, and then head 50 miles west to Murphy Hot Springs on a paved two-lane road. The route via Bruneau is gravel all the way; there are no services anywhere between Bruneau and Murphy Hot Springs Locals carry two spare tires and a set of tools for trips on the rough road. Be aware that when it rains hard in the desert, the dirt roads turn to a quicksand-like "gumbo."

Directions to North Access: Follow the Clover-Three Creek Road south of Bruneau approximately 20 miles to an (unsigned) two-way junction just inside the Saylor Creek Bombing Range boundary. This junction with the Centennial Trail is about four miles south of the signed turnoff to the Bruneau Canyon overlook. It's also about eight miles north of Clover Creek (East Fork) crossing. Head dead south on the primitive jeep road.

Best supply points: Mountain Home or Twin Falls. In a pinch: Murphy Hot Springs, Three Creek, Rogerson or Bruneau.

Trail description: Here you are, at the beginning of the southern terminus of the Idaho Centennial Trail. For long-distance travelers, this is where you take a big step out of civilized life into the vast unknown of a 1,200-mile, big-time adventure in the wild Idaho outback. We wish you luck and good fortune. This section of the Centennial Trail features an overland journey through lots of rocky, sagebrush

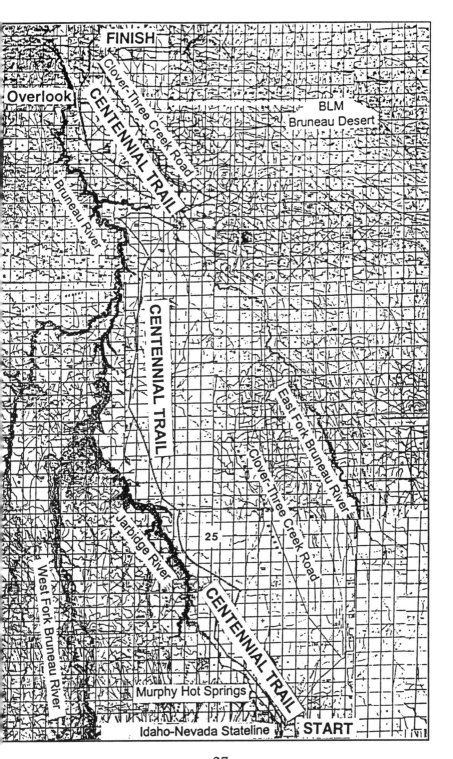

terrain alongside two breathtaking river canyons, the Jarbidge and the Bruneau. Although the entire route tilts downhill (5,991 to 3,500 feet above sea level), the undulating terrain will not necessarily feel like a downhill cruise for human-powered travelers. This is big, wide-open country, with practically no shade and lots of wind. Rest assured, you will feel as if you're in the desert when the summer

Roger Williams

The Jarbidge River canyon cuts a deep and impressive swath through rhyolite lava flows.

heat kicks into high gear in June. When it's cold, however, the wind can cut through your body like a knife. Before you begin, be sure to stock up on lots of water for a potentially hot, windy and dusty experience in the southern Idaho desert. The beginning of the Centennial Trail lies on the Idaho-Nevada border, about four miles south of Murphy Hot Springs. It's probably best to drive to Murphy Hot Springs the night before

your journey begins for a soothing soak at the homespun resort. **Be sure to call ahead for reservations, 208-857-2233, if you plan to stay overnight; rooms are limited.** It is possible to complete this section of the Centennial Trail with vehicle support the entire way.

To begin, drive south from the Murphy Hot Springs airstrip to a barbed-wire fence and a small bullet-hole sign indicating the Idaho-Nevada border (the sign may or may not be present). Jarbidge Mountain rises impressively to the south. This is the beginning of the Idaho Centennial Trail, (elev. 5,991) on the primitive dirt road. Head north on the road back to the airstrip. Avoid the turnoff to the hot springs resort, and head north on a primitive road that runs parallel to the east side of the Jarbidge River canyon. It's possible to walk or ride horseback along the canyon rim for a more scenic view, but there is no trail per se on the rim. Motorized vehicles and mountain bikes should remain on the primitive road to avoid damaging the fragile desert soil. About 12 miles north of the border, the primitive road bends away from the Jarbidge Canyon and follows a trajectory for Poison Butte (elev. 5,676 feet). The road will bend back toward the canyon, so cross-country hikers and equestrians may want to stay along the rim to save time and energy. Just east of the butte, the primitive road comes to a three-way junction. Turn left and proceed straight through the next intersection. At the next three-way junction, bear left and follow the trail in a northwest bead for the Jarbidge Canyon. It's about 10 miles now to the Poison Creek canyon, a fine spot to fetch water and make camp.

28

Proceeding on from the Poison Creek rim, head north on the primitive two-track road in the direction of Inside Lakes, which likely will be dry. If you're hiking or riding horseback along the Jarbidge Canyon, it's about eight miles from Poison Creek to the turnoff to Indian Hot Springs, where the Jarbidge joins the West Fork of the Bruneau River to form the main Bruneau River Canyon. Indian Hot Springs is a launch point for whitewater boaters who float this highly scenic 35-mile canyon. Motorized trail users may want to take a side trip down to Indian Hot Springs as a place to soak or camp. The primitive road dropping into the Bruneau Canyon is a very steep "rock garden." Continuing north, the primitive road heads almost in a straight bead to the north. In a couple miles, you'll pass a junction with a jeep trail that heads toward Stiff Tree Draw, a possible camp spot. Then, you'll pass through Sheepstead Draw, where you

Roger Williams

Great Basin rattlesnakes are a frequent sight in the Owyhee Desert.

may find a water spring. There are several side roads in Sheepstead Draw that head over to the Bruneau Canyon for a beautiful view of the deep chasm. About five miles north of Sheepstead Draw, the trail veers to the left at a two-way, Y-junction near Lookout Butte. Now it's about four miles to Twin Lakes, a mile before the East Fork canyon, also known as Clover Creek. At the Twin Lakes junction, hikers and horseback riders should head straight and follow an old wagon road to the East Fork, and rejoin the Centennial Trail two miles north of the crossing. You can save eight miles with this detour. Other trail users should turn right at the Twin Lakes junction and follow the main road four miles to Winter Camp, a private ranch where the East Fork meanders through a meadow. This is a rare place that's flat enough to cross the East Fork. The landowner has granted permission to cross through his property, please tread lightly. Cross the creek next to a wellhead and follow the trail along the right side of the East Fork for about 1.5 miles. Then the trail exits the canyon by a water tank and heads northwest on the rim. It's about 10 miles from the East Fork crossing to Big Draw, a potential camping spot. There is a trail from Big Draw into the Bruneau Canyon, if you're running short on water. It's a big drop into the canyon, though, and a steep climb out. The Bruneau Canyon overlook is about three miles to the north, and the Clover-Three Creek road is four miles north.

Historical and interpretive notes: In the early 1900s, **Murphy Hot Springs** was known as "Kitty's Hot Hole." It was named for Kitty Wilkins, who had one of the largest horse ranches in the West. She sold mounts to the U.S. Cavalry, and she headquartered at Kitty's Hot Hole.... **The Jarbidge River** was named by Shoshone Indians, according to *Idaho Place Names.* The word means "devil" or "monster," indicating the canyon must have been a bit of a nemesis to the Indians.... The **Bruneau River** was called "Rocky Bluff Creek" by early trappers.

#2 Clover-Three Cr. Rd. to Glenns Ferry

South access: Clover-Three Creek Road
North access: Slick Bridge on Snake River, west of Glenns Ferry
Distance: 27 miles
High point: Bruneau Canyon overlook, 3,700 feet
Low point: Snake River crossing, 2,800 feet
Type of trail: Primitive jeep trail, cross country
Uses allowed: Hiking, horseback, mountain bikes, motorcycles, ATVs, vehicles.
Terrain: High desert plateau, undulating rough and rocky terrain, creek-side terrain

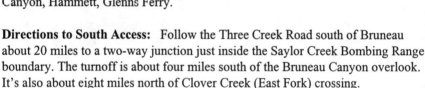

Season: Late April to early November
Access to water: Spotty; Be sure to carry plenty
Overview map: Sheep Creek, Glenns Ferry BLM map
Topo maps: Hot Spring, Bruneau Dunes, Indian Cove, Pence Butte, Pot Hole Canyon, Hammett, Glenns Ferry.

Directions to South Access: Follow the Three Creek Road south of Bruneau about 20 miles to a two-way junction just inside the Saylor Creek Bombing Range boundary. The turnoff is about four miles south of the Bruneau Canyon overlook. It's also about eight miles north of Clover Creek (East Fork) crossing.

Directions to North Access: Take Interstate 84 to the Hammett exit (about 10 miles west of Glenns Ferry) and head east on Idaho 78-U.S. 30, a two-lane paved road, toward Glenns Ferry. It's about six miles to the Slick Bridge across the Snake River.

Caution: <u>Be sure to stock up on water for a potentially hot, windy and dusty trip through the southern Idaho desert. Carry a water purifier for treating river water or spring water.</u>

Trail description: This section of the Centennial Trail travels through a mixture of public and private land as the route descends from the Bruneau desert into the foothills above Glenns Ferry and the Snake River, and crosses the Snake at Slick Bridge, a couple miles west of Glenns Ferry. Depending on your mode of travel, you may want to bypass some of the route in the foothills above the Snake and take Idaho 78 to Slick Bridge. From the Clover-Three Creek road, head northeast on a primitive two-track road for 1.5 miles, then head dead north on the primitive road through about five miles of the northern part of the Saylor Creek Bombing Range. You may see an Air Force sign that says "Air Force Bombing Range; Travel at your own risk." Rest assured that you're not traveling inside an actual target zone, so you shouldn't see any jets dropping dummy bombs nearby, but you may get buzzed by

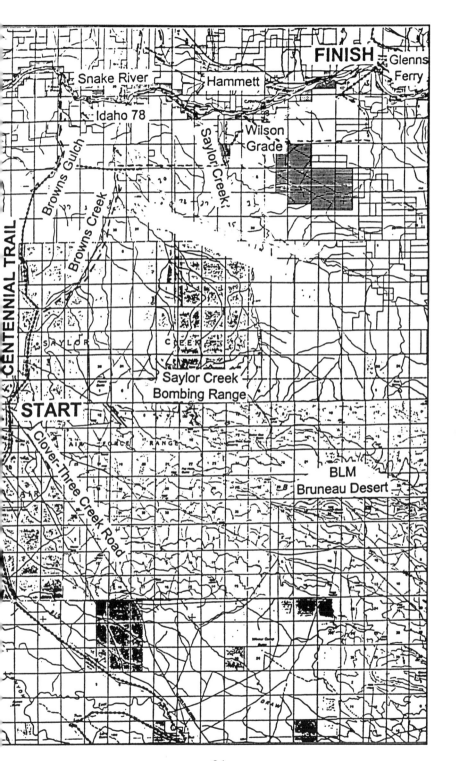

a jet flying less than 100 feet above the ground. On the northern boundary of the bombing range, the primitive road drops into Browns Gulch and continues along the gulch for about six miles. Just before Browns Gulch road passes by a gate and a sheep corral, consider turning right and dropping down an even more primitive 2-track road into Browns Creek. Both Browns Gulch and Browns Creek are dry washes, with no dependable water. Browns Gulch road dumps out on Idaho 78. Take the highway east to the Slick Bridge, if you chose that route Browns Creek

Leo Hennessy

The author rides through a band of sheep in Browns Creek.

drops into the lower valley. About eight miles from the sheep corral, the road takes a hard right-hand turn and bee-lines to the east. Shortly after the right-hand bend, the Pot Hole Road turns off to the left and heads to Idaho 78. Hikers and equestrian may want to continue straight, in an easterly direction, for Saylor Creek. The gravel road rises to a hill, within sight of the Saylor Creek canyon, and there's a gate on the left. Turn left through the gate (you're on public land here), and then drop into Saylor Creek , as you see fit. The big canyon has no well-worn trail dropping down from the top, and the draws are chock-full of tumbleweeds. Hence, this portion is only suitable for hikers, horses, llamas and goats. At the bottom of Saylor Creek, turn left and head down-canyon to the mouth, and then bear right on the old Oregon Trail toward the Wilson Grade. Follow the Oregon Trail gravel road on the flat next to the Snake River for about two miles, and then climb up the Wilson Grade to the top of some irrigated farms. The turn to the Wilson grade may be marked by an interpretive sign. When you crest the top of the foothills, follow a gravel two-track road at the top in a southerly direction for about 100 yards, and then turn left on a well-traveled gravel two-track road. This is called the West Saylor Creek Road. It goes straight for about five miles to a T-junction with a paved road. Turn left and follow the paved road a couple miles down into the valley to the Snake River crossing at Slick Bridge.

If you headed down Browns Gulch to Idaho 78, it's possible to take a public road on the south side of the Snake River, just before the Indian Cove Bridge, and follow it toward the Oregon Trail and the Wilson Grade. There is one private ranch that you'll encounter along the way. Ask for permission to cross, if you're inclined to

ake that route.
After crossing
through the ranch
on a two-track
road, you'll
intersect the trail
merging from
Taylor Creek, and
continue east
toward the
Wilson Grade.
Hikers may want
to try to follow
the southern route
of the Oregon
Trail, and avoid
climbing up the
hill. But there is
no trail through

Stephen Stuebner

A person can almost get knocked over by afternoon high winds on the Snake River at Slick Bridge. Here, a backlit Leo Hennessy manages to stay on his feet.

the Narrows of the Snake, and there is some private land along the riverside route. You'll see the Wilson Grade climbing out of the Snake River canyon to irrigated farms on top of the bench. Follow the previous directions for Browns Creek travelers to finish the trip through the farm country.

Historical and interpretive notes: The Bruneau River was called "Rocky Bluff Creek" by early trappers, according to *Idaho Place Names.* Capt. Bonneville's 1837 map of the Snake River territory called it the Powder River. John Work's journal referred to the Bruneau River in 1931, perhaps naming the river for a French-Canadian trapper named Baptiste Bruneau. There also was an Indian named "Bruneau John," who hung out in the lower Bruneau Valley near the present-day townsite of Bruneau. Bruneau John apparently warned Mountain Home white residents to stay away from the Bruneau Valley during the Bannock Indian uprising in 1878, saving their lives. All of the major land features in this area carry the name Bruneau, including the local hot springs near town, the Bruneau Valley, and the Bruneau Sand Dunes... On Idaho 78, you can head west and **take a detour to Bruneau Dunes State Park** for a shower, camping or a side hike. The Dunes are 470 feet high. The Dunes occupy an ancient meander of the Snake River; they began to accumulate about 30,000 years ago, following the aftermath of the Bonneville Flood.

Fish and critters: Travelers on the Centennial Trail likely will see cattle or domestic sheep grazing on the desert plateau, as well as antelope, coyotes and deer.

#3 Glenns Ferry to U.S. 20

North access: U.S. 20, N. of Mountain
Home
South access: Slick Bridge, near Glenns
Ferry
Distance: 35 miles
High point: Bennett Mountain crossing,
6,765 feet
Low point: Snake River crossing, 2,800 feet
Type of trail: Primitive jeep trail, cross
country
Uses allowed: Hiking, horseback, mountain
bikes, motorcycles, ATVs, vehicles
Terrain: Long and steep 4,000-foot vertical
climb from Snake River canyon through
desert grasslands, basalt canyons and bluffs to a mountain forest trail.
Season: Late April to early November
Access to water: Good in wet months, spotty in mid-summer
Overview map: Glenns Ferry and Mountain Home BLM maps
Topo maps: Glenns Ferry, Morrow Reservoir, Hot Springs Creek Reservoir,
Bennett Mountain, Goodman Flat

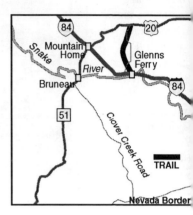

Directions to South Access: Take Interstate 84 to the Hammett exit (about 10
miles west of Glenns Ferry) and head east on Idaho 78-U.S. 30, a two-lane paved
road, toward Glenns Ferry. It's about six miles to the Slick Bridge across the Snake
River.

Directions to North Access: Take I-84 to the Mountain Home-Sun Valley exit
(U.S. 20). Go north on U.S. 20 about 20 miles to a right-hand turnoff to Little
Canyon Creek Road. The turn comes up on a sharp left-hand bend in the road,
about three miles past Little Camas Reservoir. The Centennial Trail runs along
Little Canyon Road until it crosses over Bennett Mountain.

Best resupply points: Glenns Ferry or Mountain Home. Both Elmore County
towns have full-service grocery stores, hotels, restaurants and service stations.
Glenns Ferry is the only convenient choice for long-distance travelers because the
town is so close to the Centennial Trail. By virtue of being a larger town and an Air
Force base, Mountain Home has more stores, fast-food restaurants, nicer hotels and
a major truck stop on I-84 — even a K-Mart!

Caution: <u>Be sure to stock up on water for a potentially hot, windy and dusty trip in
the southern Idaho desert. Carry a water purifier for treating river water or spring
water.</u>

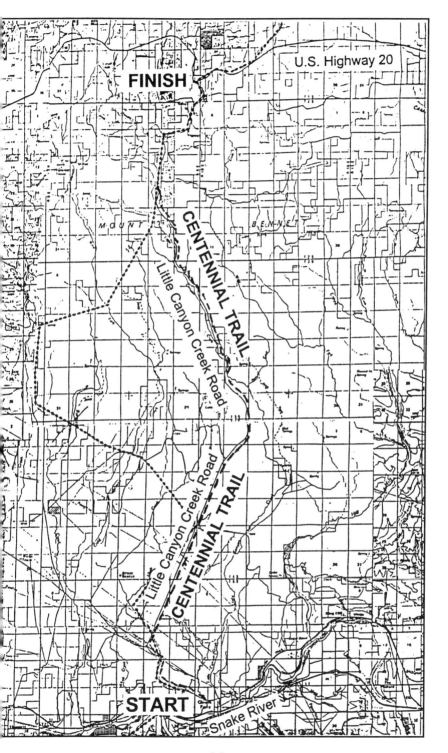

Trail description: We will describe two ways for people to travel from Glenns Ferry to U.S. 20, a quick way through, all on 2WD dirt road open to all uses, via the Little Canyon Creek road. It's also possible for hikers and horseback riders to follow a very circuitous route along the original Centennial Trail route, but we do not recommend it because there is no trail in places, and there are several places where it crosses or skirts private land. **To hook up with the Little Canyon Creek Road,** head into Glenns Ferry from the Slick Bridge. It's about two miles east to the outskirts of Glenns Ferry. Turn left and follow the road under the Interstate for less than a half-mile to a left-hand junction. Turn left and follow the road in a northwesterly direction about four miles to a major junction with Little Canyon Creek Road. Turn right and head past Morrow Reservoir and cruise up the road. It' about 34 miles on the major dirt road, nearly all of it slightly uphill. Then, after you cross the back-shoulder of Bennett Mountain, it's downhill to U.S. 20, the end of this trail segment.

The original Centennial Trail route is only suitable for foot travel or light stock travel because there is no trail tread in many places. The route proceeds north from Slick Bridge to the irrigation canal directly above. There is a path along the canal that takes you across the freeway and then to the east until a jeep trail intersects the canal road from the north. Turn left on the jeep trail and head north for about a mile. At the first four-way junction, turn left on a 2WD dirt road. Stay on the road as it weaves into the lower foothills of Bennett Mountain. In about five miles, the 2WD road comes to a junction with Alkali Creek, a right-hand turnoff for the Centennial Trail. The turnoff is about one mile past the point where the powerline crosses over the top of the road next to a creek crossing. Head up a mini-basalt canyon along Alkali Creek for about two miles. There is no trail in the creek bottom. When the canyon bends to the north, climb out of the draw, cross over a small bluff, and drop into a parallel draw. Again, there is no trail. The trail climbs a a gradual pace for about two miles to a small reservoir. Just before the reservoir, peel left and begin a 5-mile overland cruise to Ryegrass Creek. Pick your own route because there is no trail. At a junction with Ryegrass Creek, there's a two-way road intersection just above the west bank of the creek. Take the road that heads west-northwest (don't go north along Ryegrass Creek), and in two miles, you'll come to a major ranch road. Turn right and follow the road for less than a quarter-mile. Take the next right, a single-lane dirt road. Head north on the road as it snakes up a bluff overlooking Bennett Creek. In three miles, the Centennial Trail peels away from the dirt road by a spring, and a switchback.... Now the Centennial Trail heads up the slope of Bennett Mountain. There is no trail, and you may run into private land on Bennett Mountain. Please ask for permission and tread lightly. You'll pass over a timbered saddle at 6,765 feet, and then down the north slope of Bennett Mountain to Little Canyon Creek Road, a major ranch road. The trail crosses upper Ryegrass Creek just below the saddle, and then it crosses Cold Springs Creek before the trail makes a lovely descent from the Bennett Mountain saddle to a lower shoulder ridge for about three miles in a forested setting. Then, the trail intersects Little Canyon Creek Road. Turn left on the 2WD ranch road. It's about seven miles to the junction with U.S. 20.

Historical and interpretive notes: Three Mile Island Crossing State Park, just a mile or so down the road toward Glenns Ferry from the Slick Bridge, is a full-service campground (make reservations in the high season) with water. The park's location is a historical site, the actual crossing that Oregon Trail emigrants used 1840-1860. The crossing was somewhat treacherous, involving deep points in the rushing Snake River where horses and oxen had to swim as they led the wagons across. Every summer, the crossing is re-enacted by rugged locals, who dress up like the emigrants and ride horse-drawn wagons across the Snake at Three Island Crossing, a courageous feat to be sure ... **Glenns Ferry** is named for Gustavus P. Glenn, who ran a ferry service across the Snake River from 1865-1889. The first Post Office was established in 1879; the town formed four years later ... **A series of islands** on the Snake River in the Glenns Ferry area play home to a wide variety of birds, wildlife and waterfowl. It's a wonderful place to paddle a canoe (watch out for the huge afternoon headwinds), or hunt pheasants and waterfowl by boat.

Fish and critters: Encounters with cattle grazing in the foothills of Bennett Mountain will likely be frequent, depending on the time of year. Please respect private property and don't chase livestock. Watch for chukar and Hungarian partridge, forest grouse, antelope, coyotes and deer. There are no trout fishing areas of note in this section of the Centennial Trail, because the streams are only intermittent in the lower foothills, and the upper creeks, such as Cold Springs Creek, and Ryegrass Creek just don't have many fish in them.

#4 U.S. 20 to Willow Cr. Campground

South access: U.S. 20, near Little Camas Reservoir
North access: Willow Creek Campground, near Featherville
Distance: 38 miles
High point: Grouse Butte, 7,656 feet
Low point: High Prairie junction, 5,445
Type of trail: 2WD dirt road, primitive jeep trail, single-track trail
Uses allowed: Hiking, horseback, mountain bikes, motorcycles (portions open to ATVs)
Terrain: High sagebrush prairie, steep mountain terrain in forested setting.
Season: late May to early October

Access to water: Good in forested route; poor in first 10 miles of trail
Overview map: Sawtooth National Forest, Fairfield Ranger District
Topo maps: Cat Creek Summit, High Prairie, Sprout Mountain, Grouse Butte.

Directions to South Access: Take I-84 to the Mountain Home-Sun Valley exit (U.S. 20). Go east on U.S. 20 about 24 miles to a signed left-hand turnoff for Forest Highway 61, the main road to Pine and Featherville. Turn left on FH 61 and park. The Centennial Trail proceeds north on this wide 2WD paved road.

Directions to North Access: Take I-84 to the Mountain Home-Sun Valley exit (U.S. 20). Go north on U.S. 20 about 24 miles to a signed left-hand turnoff for Forest Highway 61, the main road to Pine and Featherville. Turn left on FH 61 and follow it to Pine and Featherville. It's a lovely drive along Anderson Ranch Reservoir, and then a series of meadows (great car-camping areas) along the South Fork of the Boise River to the old gold-mining town of Featherville. Drive through town, and turn right on USFS Road #227. Proceed about seven miles to the Willow Creek Campground, a no-fee site with a toilet.

Best resupply points: Mountain Home. In a pinch: Pine or Featherville, both small towns with cafes and small supply stores, have some basic items. An Air Force base, Mountain Home has grocery stores, department stores, fast-food restaurants, nicer hotels and a major truck stop on I-84 — even a K-Mart!

Caution: Carry a water purifier for treating water.

Trail description: Beginning from the junction of U.S. 20 and Forest Highway 61, proceed north on FH 61. Go straight through the next four-way junction in two miles, and head for Moore's Spring. Bear right at a three-junction by the spring, and follow USFS Road #181. This is a 2WD dirt road that provides access to several

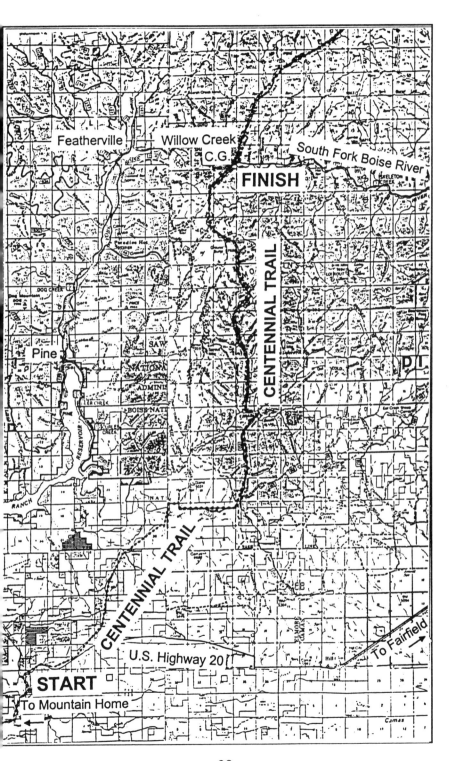

Featherville
Willow Creek
C.G.
South Fork Boise River
FINISH
CENTENNIAL TRAIL
Pine
D.L.
BOISE NAT.
RESERVOIR
RANCH
CENTENNIAL TRAIL
To Fairfield
U.S. Highway 20
START
To Mountain Home

ranches in high wind-swept meadows, on the edge of the Camas Prairie. The camas blooms here are legendary in May and early June. It's about seven miles on #181 to a junction with USFS Road #055 next to Cow Creek. From this point north, you're in the Sawtooth National Forest. Turn left on #055 and follow it for 3.5 miles to a point where the road ends at the Hunter Creek trailhead and transfer camp. Here, the trail turns into single-track. Nearby, the south, north and middle forks of Lime Creek join to form Lime Creek, a good fishing stream. The Centennial Trail proceeds up the South Fork of Lime Creek for about a mile, and then branches off to join the Middle Fork of Lime Creek. You are now traveling on the west flank of the Soldier Mountains, a range that forms a divide between the Camas Prairie and the South Fork of the Boise River. Cross the Middle Fork ford and proceed to a trail junction sign. Turn left at the junction and head for the North Fork of Lime Creek, which is about one mile away. As an alternative to the North Fork trail, a high ridge trail called the Presidents Trail may be preferable for motorcyclists and mountain bikers. The trail along the North Fork of Lime Creek is usually cleared each year, but it's steep and technical in places. There's good fishing along here in mid-summer. Near the head of the North Fork of Lime Creek, the single-track trail yields to a primitive two-track logging road. In a mile, you'll rejoin the High Trail (trail #44) Continue to climb to the head of the creek and wrap around the back shoulder of Grouse Butte (elev. 7,656), the high point of this section. Enjoy broad views of the west side of the Soldier Mountains, the Trinities, Steel Mountain, the Smoky Mountains, the Sawtooths, and the upper South Fork Boise River country. The Centennial Trail remains on the ridge behind Grouse Butte for several miles until you come to a high saddle. Then, the trail bails into Virginia Gulch at a fairly steep pitch three miles downhill to the South Fork of the Boise River, where a bridge provides safe crossing of the river. The Willow Creek Campground is across the road, if you plan to continue on the Centennial Trail. You ought to plan on soaking in Baumgartner Hot Springs in the popular Baumgartner Campground, 3.5 miles to the east, to soothe your aching body.

Historical and interpretive notes: The beginning of this section of the Centennial Trail is an **old sheep driveway** in the high, wind-swept prairie. A few sheep ranchers still run sheep through the area in the spring and fall, as evidenced by the tell-tale cook tents used by sheepherders, which sometimes stand out as a dot on the horizon. Portions of this area also are used for cattle grazing... The **Soldier Mountains** are named for the soldiers from the U.S. Cavalry who were stationed in the Camas Prairie during the **Bannock War** in 1878. The Bannock War was triggered, at least in part, on white settlers who developed homesteads in the Camas Prairie. Bannock Indians had traditionally harvested camas bulbs in the prairie for eons. Then, the Bannock, also known as the Northern Paiute, noticed that the settlers' pigs were eating the bulbs, and that was enough to start the war on May 30, 1878. The bloodshed started with the killing of two ranchers on the Camas Prairie. The war continued throughout the summer of 1878, as the U.S. Cavalry chased the Bannock Indians to the Bruneau Valley, South Mountain in the Owyhee Mountains, where Chief Buffalo Horn was killed, and to the Blue Mountains, where the

40

The South Fork of the Boise River, near Willow Creek, is a good spot for canoeing and fishing.

Bannocks ran out of steam. According to Dick d'Easum's account in the *Idaho Statesman*, the last of the hostile Bannocks were captured in Yellowstone National Park in September. At least 40 whites had been killed, and an unknown number of Bannock Indians. But it was the last major Indian war on the Snake Plain, and from that point forward, the Shoshone and Bannock tribes were confined to the Fort Hall Reservation, north of Pocatello and west of Blackfoot.... **Portions of Lime Creek** were proposed for special recreation protection in a wilderness bill co-sponsored by former Gov. Cecil Andrus and Sen. James McClure in the late 1980s. The bill fizzled in Congress.

Fish and critters: Good trout fishing in Lime Creek. Fishing in Anderson Ranch Reservoir. Trophy trout fishing on the South Fork of the Boise River. Watch for chukar and hungarian partridge, forest grouse, antelope, coyotes, deer, elk, black bear, mountain lions, redtail hawks, rough-legged hawks and golden eagles.

Notes on geology of Soldier Mountains: The Soldier Mountains, which rise dramatically several thousand feet above the Camas Prairie, are underpinned by one of the southern-most intrusions of the Idaho Batholith, a homogenous granitic formation that dominates most of central Idaho.

#5 Willow Cr. C.G.-Mattingly Cr. Divide

South access: Willow Creek Campground, near Featherville
North access: Atlanta, west portal of Sawtooth Wilderness, or Alturas Lake Road #205 and Alturas Lake Trail #034.
Distance: 30 miles
High point: 8,816 feet
Low point: Willow Creek Campground, 5,450 feet
Type of trail: All single-track
Uses allowed: Hiking, horseback, mountain bikes, motorcycles on Willow Creek
Terrain: Forested mountain terrain, alpine meadows, creek-side trails.
Season: Early June to early October
Access to water: Excellent
Overview map: Boise National Forest, Sawtooth National Forest
Topo maps: Grouse Butte, Cayuse Point, Ross Peak, Marshall Peak, Mt. Everly, Atlanta East.

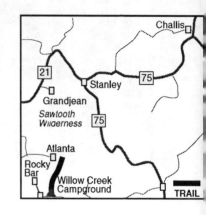

Directions to South Access: Take I-84 to the Mountain Home-Sun Valley exit (U.S. 20). Go north on U.S. 20 about 24 miles to a signed left-hand turnoff for Forest Highway 61, the main paved road to Pine and Featherville. Turn left and follow FH #61 to Pine and Featherville. It's a lovely drive along Anderson Ranch Reservoir, and then a series of meadows (great car-camping areas) along the South Fork of the Boise River to the old gold-mining town of Featherville. Drive through town, and turn right on USFS Road #227. Proceed about seven miles to the Willow Creek Campground, a no-fee campground with a toilet and campsites.

Directions to North Access: There are two possible access points from the north; neither are direct: Atlanta, on the west side of the Sawtooth Wilderness, or Alturas Lake. Atlanta can be reached via the Middle Fork Boise River Road USFS #268 from Lucky Peak Reservoir (60 miles of bone-chattering dirt road), or by taking the Edna Creek Road from Idaho 21. If you're driving from Boise, we recommend taking the Edna Creek Road to Atlanta. This route begins about 60 miles east of Boise on Idaho 21 (the turnoff is after the Whoop-Em-Up cross-country ski trailhead and parking lot. The Edna Creek Road (USFS #348) drops into the North Fork of the Boise River, then follows #327 as it climbs into the Middle Fork, and then #268 to Atlanta. The Centennial Trail is 4.5 miles up the Middle Fork Boise River trail, where it intersects with Mattingly Creek. Climb about seven miles along the Mattingly Creek Trail to the Divide (8,816 feet). To reach Alturas Lake, follow Idaho 75 to the well-marked turnoff for Alturas Lake, about 22 miles south of Stanley. Follow the paved road around the north side of the lake and continue on

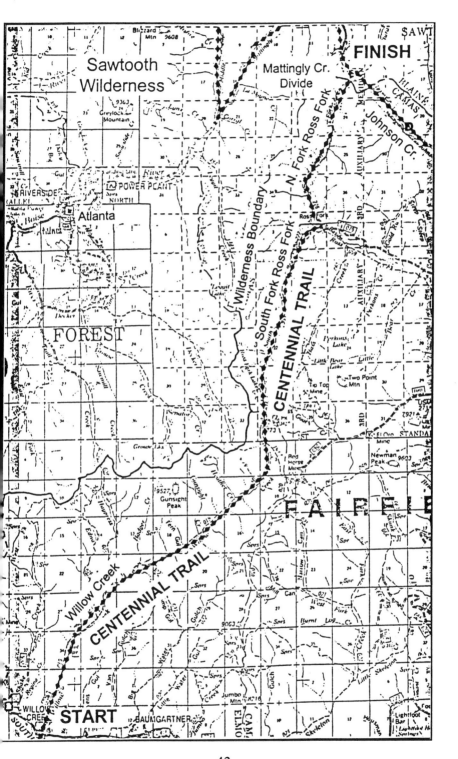

USFS Road #205 to the Alturas Lake Creek Trailhead. Then, it's about three miles of trail up Trail #034 to the Mattingly Creek Divide.

Best resupply points: Mountain Home. Idaho City. In a pinch: Atlanta, a small town with a cafe and a couple of bars, has some basic items.

Leo Hennessy

A wooden bridge provides safe crossing of the South Fork of the Boise River near the Willow Creek Campground.

Caution: Carry a water purifier for treating water.

Trail description: Beginning from theWillow Creek Campground, head north on the Willow Creek Road 1.5 miles to the Willow Creek Transfer Camp and the Willow Creek trailhead. The trail is a well-maintained single-track trail #019. It's a long climb, a hefty 4,200-foot vertical rise to a high pass next to Ross Peak (elev. 9,774 feet). It's about 12 miles to the saddle, with several creek-crossings. Watch for a hot springs about two miles up the trail. Some hikers have placed a tarp in the rocks to dam up the springs. It's a very scenic climb up a series of mountain meadows along Willow Creek. Great views of the big granite outcroppings and peaks in the distance make this a very scenic trail. At the saddle, consider a sidehike to Ross Peak for a great view, or possibly an evening bivouac. The Ross Fork Lakes, below the saddle, may be the best place for a midway camp. Continuing on, the Centennial Trail drops into the uppermost headwaters of the South Fork of the Boise River. You'll descend from the top of the pass on the upper South Fork of the South Fork trail #227 into the Ross Fork Basin. This would be another nice place to camp. Then, the trail climbs out of the basin via the North Fork of the South Fork trail #226. It's a big haul, about seven miles, from the Ross Fork Basin to a high saddle and ridge complex leading to the Sawtooth Wilderness boundary. At the next junction on the high saddle, you'll hook up with trail #034, which leads to the Sawtooth Wilderness and the headwaters of Mattingly Creek at 8,816 feet. At this high point, you're perched above the southern region of the Sawtooth Wilderness. A sea of granite peaks unfolds before your eyes, including Mattingly Peak. Mountain bikers and motorcyclists can make a quick exit from

Roger Williams

As the Centennial Trail heads north into the Ross Fork Basin, just south of the Sawtooths, the peaks and ridges get more dramatic.

his point by turning right on the Alturas Lake Creek Trail #034 and descending about eight miles to Alturas Lake, via the single-track trail, and then Alturas Lake Creek Creek Road #205 to Idaho Highway 75. Then, of course, you'll need to hook up with a shuttle driver to take you back home. To head back to Atlanta, follow Trail #034 from the head of Mattingly Creek down the right side of Mattingly Creek. The trail crosses the creek three times before it comes to a junction with the Middle Fork Boise River Trail #460. The last crossing is the most difficult during spring runoff. Then continue on Trail #460 into Atlanta.

Historical and interpretive notes: Willow Creek Campground is near several areas that were extensively mined for gold in the late 1800s and early 1900s. **Featherville** was heavily dredge-mined in the 1920s, as the many piles of river cobble adjacent to the little mountain town can attest. In *Idaho Place Names,* Lalia Boone reports that about 33,000 ounces of gold were extracted from the Featherville area from 1922 to 1927. A Post Office operated in the town from 1906 to 1928.... **Rocky Bar**, which is a ghost town today, was worked in the first years of the gold rush, in 1863 ...**Gold was discovered in the Atlanta area** in 1864. Mining continued there until the 1930s. Several large mining corporations have threatened to develop a large open-pit mine in the Atlanta area, but so far, that has not occurred.... **You'll encounter several natural hot springs in Atlanta** for a soothing soak.

#6 Mattingly Cr. Divide to Stanley Lake

South access: Atlanta, ID, or Alturas Lake.
North access: Stanley Lake Trailhead #640
Distance: 31.5
High point: 8,890 feet
Low point: 5,200 feet
Type of Trail: All single-track wilderness trail
Uses allowed: Hikers, stock users
Terrain: Rugged mountain terrain with many alpine lakes, granite boulders, scree slopes and cobble, mountain streams and forest.
Season: July to early October
Access to water: Excellent. Many streams and lakes. Purify all water.
Overview map: Hiking Map and Guide for Sawtooth Wilderness, or Sawtooth National Forest map.
Topo maps: Grandjean, Edaho Mountain, Warbonnet Peak, Mt. Everly, Atlanta East, Snowyside Peak

Directions to South Access: Atlanta, the west gateway of the Sawtooth Wilderness, can be reached from access points near Boise, Idaho City, Mountain Home and Featherville. Follow a Boise National Forest map for details on dirt roads to Atlanta. Drive by the Whistlestop bar and cafe and head for the Power Plant Trailhead. Follow Trail #460 along the Middle Fork of Boise River for 4.5 miles to the Mattingly Creek junction in the Sawtooth Wilderness. Or, take Idaho 75 to the well-marked turnoff for Alturas Lake, about 22 miles south of Stanley. Go up the Alturas Lake Road #205 and take Trail #034 to the Mattingly Creek Divide. Then, descend along Mattingly Creek to the Middle Fork Trail #460 and pick up the Centennial Trail here.

Directions to North Access: From Stanley, ID, take Idaho Highway 21 about six miles west of Stanley to the well-marked turnoff for Stanley Lake. Turn onto the bumpy 2WD gravel road to the Stanley Lake trailhead at the far end of the lake.

Best Supply Points: Stanley. Atlanta has very limited supplies. Grandjean Lodge does not have supplies.

Trail description: The rugged beauty of the Sawtooth Mountain Range makes this section of the Idaho Centennial Trail one of the most scenic and spectacular in the state. As the Centennial Trail cuts north through the heart of the Sawtooth Wilderness, it passes through jagged mountains amd picturesque streams and lakes. You won't see a dirt road until Grandjean. **To begin,** pick up Trail #460 as it intercepts the Centennial Trail at the junction with the Mattingly Creek Trail #034. It's nine

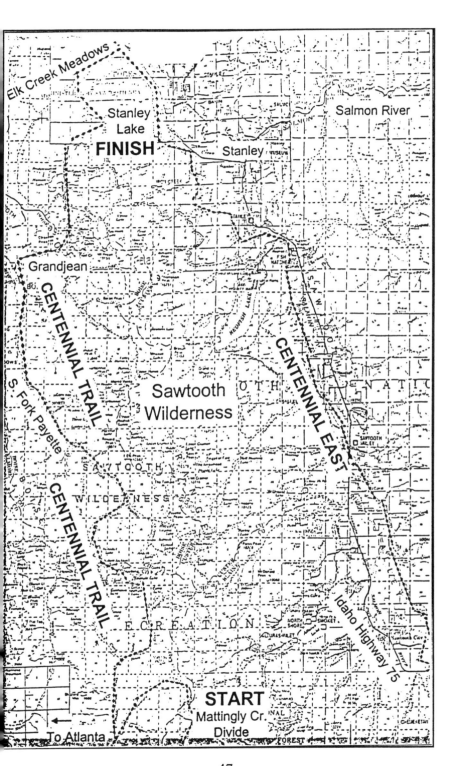

miles to the Spangle Lakes. Cross Mattingly Creek and continue along the east side of the Middle Fork Boise River to the first river ford just beyond where Rock Creek enters the river from the west (3.5 mi., 6,400 ft.). This ford can be made in two stages but may be difficult early in the summer. Keep to the right along the river at the trail junction to Timpa Lake. After passing through open brush slopes, the trail crosses the river three times as the granite walls of the river close in on it. If you are lucky, you can find logs at these crossings. The trail crosses twice more where the river levels and spreads out a half mile below Flytrip Creek and trail (7.5 miles, 7,400 feet). Keep left (west) at the trail junction and begin an incredible series of short switchbacks up the face of a ridge to 8,000 ft. Another good mile brings you past the outlet to Little Spangle Lake and to the junction with Centennial Trail #462 and #463 to Ardith Lake (9 miles, 8500 ft.) The Spangle Lakes are jewels of the Sawtooths. They are not as heavily used as some lakes and have a number of good campsites. Glenn's peak which watches over them is an easy climb. **Proceeding on,** follow Trail #462 from Spangle Lake to the South Fork Payette River (7.5 miles). The trail follows beautiful turquoise Spangle Lake, crosses the outlet to Little Spangle, climbs switchbacks to a small lake, and continues up to Lake Ingeborg. The trail provides excellent views of the Spangle Lakes and Glenns Peak, with Snowyside and Flytrip Basin in the distance. Ingeborg Lake (one mile, 8,890 feet) is an exquisite emerald lake sitting on a saddle between the Boise River and Payette River drainages. Spectacular North and South Raker peaks can be seen to the west. Spend some time here before heading down switchbacks to Rockslide Lake, named for the boulder fields across the lake. The trail continues downward through woods passing above a shallow lake and boggy meadows. An indistinct and unmarked trail comes in from Three Island Lake at the lower end of this area. Soon you will see Benedict Lake. The trail is above the lake but drops down to its edge near the outlet (12.5 miles, 8,200 feet). Much of the lake shore has grass and is not very accessible, but there are "leave no trace" camping spots across the outlet. This route is seldom traveled and fishing is quite good. From the lake outlet, the trail drops 1,000 feet in four miles to the South Fork of the Payette River trail, a wilderness highway. Below the switchbacks and above the junction to Queens River Trail #458, Benedict Creek glides over slab rock providing an excellent spot to rest and cool off. Below the Queens River trail outlet crossing, the trail stays on the west slopes above Benedict Creek sometimes crossing rock slides with little shade. Above the junction with Trail #452 (16.5 miles, 7,200 feet), you can get great views of the South Fork Payette River.

Turn left on Trail #452 and follow the South Fork downhill for about 15 miles to Grandjean. The trail follows the river closely through thick woods until it crosses the South Fork at 19.5 miles. It is necessary to ford the river here as there is no log or bridge. The crossing should n't be a problem after mid-July. The trail continues through woods to Elk Lake (20.5 miles) where there are several campsites. The trail continues on the north side of the river all the way to Grandjean. It drops steeply below Elk Lake and there are a number of cascades and waterfalls in addition to Fern Falls. Below this, the trail leaves the river in long gradual switchbacks. The junction of Trails #453 and #452 (continuation of Centennial Trail to the north) is about 0.1 mile from the Grandjean Trailhead (31.5 miles).

Proceeding on, take Trail #453, which climbs up the right side of Trail Creek, providing great views of the South Fork Payette River drainage. The trail passes mostly through wooded terrain crossing the creek three times in the first three miles, which can be a problem early in the summer. After crossing a small stream near the Wilderness Boundary, the trail passes through a short, steep open area, then continues in long switchbacks to the Trail Creek Lake junction (5 miles, 7,500 feet). A one mile side trip to these lakes is worthwhile and provides campsites. Continue to climb along the east slopes of the drainage passing the popular Observation Peak (9,156 feet) trail on your left (west) just before reaching the Payette/Salmon Divide (7 miles, 8,020 feet). At the divide, Trail #640, on the right (east) leads to beautiful Sawtooth Lake and the heart of the Sawtooth range. Keep to the left side of the Stanley Lake Creek drainage to find the trail heading for Stanley Lake as you descend and exit the wilderness in about a half-mile. Keep to the right

Leo Hennessy

It's possible to feel as if you're on top of the world in the Sawtooths.

as you pass the side trail to Greenback Mine (8.5 miles). Cross Stanley Lake Creek (9 miles, 7,150 feet) near the junction with Trail #624 which leads west to Elk Meadows without going past Stanley Lake. However, you'll miss the beautiful Bridal Veil Falls (10 miles, 6,800 feet). A side trip to the creek edge provides a better view of the falls. After the trail crosses the creek to the west, the trail descends on an old mining road while the creek passes over a noisy, but difficult-to-see, waterfall. The last three miles are flat and cross sunny meadows along the creek providing great views of McGowan Peak and others. Keep going down the creek as you pass the Alpine Way Trail #628 (12.5 miles) which follows the Wilderness boundary to Redfish Lake and continue to the trailhead at Stanley Lake Inlet Campground (14 miles, 6,513 ft.).

Historical and interpretive notes: The **Sawtooth Mountains** form a three-way divide between the Boise, Payette and Salmon rivers. These waters finally come together in Hells Canyon on the Idaho-Oregon border ...The Sawtooths are the most popular wilderness area in the state, with about 30,000 visitors per year.

49

#7 Mattingly Cr. Divide to ID 75 (Centennial East)

South access: North Fork of Ross Fork Trail
via Alturas Lake Creek Trail #034
North access: Highway Idaho 75 at Decker
Flats Road, near Smiley Creek
Distance: 32.5 miles
High point: 9,050 ft.
Low point: 6,300 ft
Type of trail: Single track, 4WD jeep trail
Uses allowed: Hiking, equestrian, mountain
bikes, motorcycles
Terrain: Forested mountains and streams
Season: July to October
Access to water: Excellent.
Overview map: Sawtooth National Forest
Topo maps: Marshall Peak, Frenchman Creek, Galena, Horton Peak, Alturas Lake, Obsidian

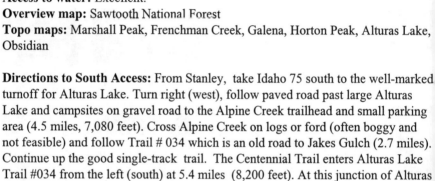

Directions to South Access: From Stanley, take Idaho 75 south to the well-marked turnoff for Alturas Lake. Turn right (west), follow paved road past large Alturas Lake and campsites on gravel road to the Alpine Creek trailhead and small parking area (4.5 miles, 7,080 feet). Cross Alpine Creek on logs or ford (often boggy and not feasible) and follow Trail # 034 which is an old road to Jakes Gulch (2.7 miles). Continue up the good single-track trail. The Centennial Trail enters Alturas Lake Trail #034 from the left (south) at 5.4 miles (8,200 feet). At this junction of Alturas Trail #034 and Ross Creek Trail #226 (5.4 miles, 8,200 feet), go left (south) on Trail #181 and head into Johnson Creek.

Directions to North Access: From Stanley, go south on Highway Idaho 75 28 miles, cross the river and turn right at the sign to the Salmon River Headwaters. Follow USFS Road #215 to Chemeketan Campground and continue on the 4WD road for 2.8 miles, crossing three streams, before reaching the trailhead at the end of the road.

Best Supply Points: Ketchum or Stanley. Smiley Creek Lodge, south of Alturas Lake Road on Idaho 75, has groceries, showers and a restaurant. Obsidian Lodge on Highway 75 north of Decker Flats Road has some groceries.

Trail Description: This section of the Centennial Trail provides an eastern alternative route around the Sawtooth Wilderness for multiple-use trail users. It is a circuitous route featuring all single-track forest trail with many stream crossings. It's also a high-elevation route that winds through the headwaters of the South Fork

51

of the Boise River and the headwaters of the Salmon River. **To begin,** pick up Trail #181 just north of the Ross Creek Divide at a three-way junction with Mattingly Creek, Alturas Lake Trail and Johnson Creek Trail. Contour to the northeast crossing back over the divide (0.5 miles, 8,435 feet) into the Johnson Creek drainage. After a couple of switchbacks, #181 continues south, meeting Johnson Creek at about 7,700 feet. Continue on the left side of Johnson Creek past the junction with Vienna Creek trail (5.5 miles, 6,700 feet). Do not take trail #086 up Vienna Creek. The trail disappears and no longer exists at the east end. Trail #181 crosses Johnson Creek to the west and then ends as it intersects Trail #079, a 4WD jeep trail, at 7.4 miles (6,300 feet). Go left (east) on the jeep trail, #079, which crosses back over Johnson Creek. Several streams come together forming the South Fork of the Boise River which you will follow downstream. It leaves the river at 6,300 feet and climbs to 6,800 feet before dropping into Emma Creek and crossing it at 11 miles.

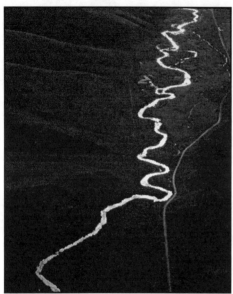

Idaho Falls Post Register

Humble beginnings: The Salmon River winds into the Sawtooth Valley near the headwaters.

Follow Trail #063 up Emma Creek. You'll cross Emma Creek once (6,600 feet), then stay on the left side of the creek to the divide. In a fairly level area, you will pass the Paradise Peak trail (7,120 feet), which heads east and crosses Emma creek. As you join an old mining road near the top, keep to the right and continue to the Divide (16.5 miles, 8,700 feet). Ignore the road to the north; it leads to private property at a mining claim. Continue on a good single-track trail which contours on the north side of the divide for about half a mile to Trail #224 at the head of the West Fork Smoky Creek. Stay on the high divide and enjoy great views north into Smiley Creek and south into the Smoky Mountains (17 miles, 9,050 feet). A new trail has been constructed to the south down the West Fork of Smoky Creek. The first switchback drops only about 600 feet. Watch closely for a small spring about one-half mile from the Divide in a heavily wooded area. Beyond the spring, the trail crosses an open area on a steep slope where you can see the trail and creek below. After two switchbacks it joins the old trail (18.8 mi., 8,200 feet) and continues down the valley on a steep, wooded hillside to the left and above the creek. Keep to the left as you pass Trail #070 (21 miles, 7,400 feet), which leads to Paradise Creek and the Big Smoky Fire Camp and pass Helen Creek Trail #074 a short distance beyond. Continue down the West Fork of Big Smoky Creek. At

52

Boggy Creek (22.2 miles), the trail may be boggy. Keep to the right down the West Fork at Trail # 198 (23.6 miles) where there is a sign and arrow. This trail leads to old mines and prospects. Good flat camping spots can be found between here and Big Smoky Creek.

Proceeding on, turn left at the junction with Trail #072 (26 miles, 6,820 feet). You will climb again now about 2,000 feet to the head of Big Smoky Creek. Follow the narrow trail upstream on the left (west) side of Big Smoky Creek. At 27.1 miles, the trail crosses the creek to the east. About a half-mile above here, the trail appears to cross to the west side then returns to the east side in about 100 feet. Both crossings are difficult, so stay on the east side if at all possible. Stay left at the trail sign for Royal Gorge, which leads to Prairie Creek Trail #196 in the Big Wood River drainage (7,000 feet). The trail again crosses Big Smoky to the west, crosses back a half-mile upstream and then continues on the east side to the divide. From here, the trail is fairly steep in open alpine country with little shade and no water. About a half mile below the divide it passes through forest and crosses a stream created by springs. The wooded divide between the Big Smoky drainage and the Salmon River (31.0 miles, 8,820 feet) is not especially scenic (in relative terms). The trail slopes to the north and skirts a large meadow full of springs which form the headwaters of the great Salmon River. Step across the Salmon "river" as it starts to tumble down into the Sawtooth Valley, and follow the trail a short distance to a well marked junction (31.4 miles). Go straight on the two-track road (closed to ATVs) which heads steeply down to the trailhead gate (32.5 miles, 7,800 feet).

Historical and interpretive notes: The Salmon River has many claims to fame. From the headwaters at Galena Summit, the river runs for more than 475 miles in a giant sweep through rugged central Idaho, carving the second-deepest canyon in Idaho and finally pouring into the Snake River in Hells Canyon on the Idaho-Oregon border. It is the longest free-flowing (dam-free) river in the lower 48 states, and the longest river that flows inside a single state in the continental United States. Remnants of the formerly abundant chinook salmon runs, the Salmon River's namesake, still spawn in a number of tributaries near the headwaters. As juveniles, the fish swim about 900 miles from central Idaho to the Pacific Ocean, and north to the Gulf of Alaska. Then, they head back home two or three years later as adults to spawn the next generation in the same stream where they were born... The Sawtooth Mountain Range has 42 peaks that rise over 10,000 feet... The Vienna Mine had a large stamp mill and produced silver and lead from 1879 to 1885. Some 200 buildings existed in the town site at one time... Sawtooth City, another old mining town near Smiley Creek, was active from 1880 to 1886. It produced an estimated $250,000 worth of minerals.

#8 ID75 to Stanley Lake
(Centennial East)

South access: South end of Headwater USFS Road #215
North access: Stanley Lake trailhead
Distance: About 50 miles
High point: 7,800 feet
Low point: 6,800 feet
Type of trail: Dirt single track, gravel 2WD roads
Uses allowed: All types, including vehicles.
Terrain: Broad open valley surrounded by spectacular mountains
Season: May to late October; plus, most areas are accessible to skiers and snowmobiles in the winter.
Access to water: Excellent
Overview map: Sawtooth National Forest
Topo maps: Frenchman Creek, Galena, Ross Peak, Alturas Lake, Obsidian, Stanley, Stanley Lake.

Directions to South Access: : From Stanley, go south on Highway Idaho 75 28 miles, cross the river and turn right (south)to the Salmon River headwaters as indicated on the highway sign. Follow USFS Road #215 to Chemeketan Campground and continue on 4WD two-track for 2.8 miles, crossing three streams, before reaching the trailhead at the end of the road.

Directions to North Access: From Stanley, go west on Idaho 21 about six miles to a well-marked turnoff for Stanley Lake. Turn left and head for Stanley Lake. The trailhead is well-marked by the lake.

Best Resupply Points: Ketchum, Hailey or Stanley. In a pinch: Smiley Creek Lodge, 3.5 miles west of the highway crossing on Idaho 75. Sessions Lodge at Obsidian, one mile north of Decker Flats Road on Idaho 75, has groceries.

Trail description: This section of Centennial East follows backcountry roads through pastoral grazing land and open range in the Sawtooth Valley, with spectacular views of the Sawtooths and White Cloud mountains throughout the route. **To begin,** head north on USFS #215, a two-track dirt road, from the gate at the Trailhead for Trail #072 (7,800 feet.). This road is not maintained for 2.5 miles, and it is suitable only for 4WD vehicles because it fords the stream three times. At Chemeketan Campground (2.8 miles), the road improves to a fairly good gravel road. You'll reach Idaho State Highway 75 at 5.8 miles. Cross over the highway and continue over a ridge on a two-track road. A gate with an Idaho Centennial

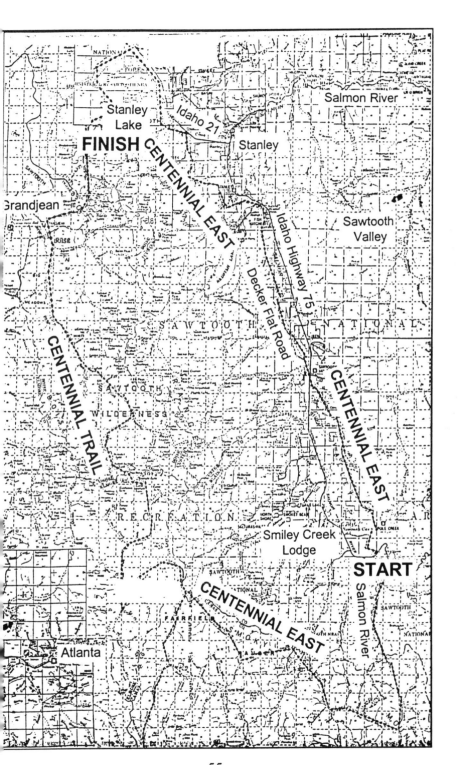

FINISH CENTENNIAL EAST

Stanley Lake

Idaho 21

Stanley

Salmon River

Grandjean

Sawtooth Valley

Idaho Highway 75

Decker Flat Road

SAWTOOTH

NATIONAL

CENTENNIAL TRAIL

SAWTOOTH WILDERNESS

CENTENNIAL EAST

RECREATION

Smiley Creek Lodge

START

Salmon River

CENTENNIAL EAST

Atlanta

Trail sign (7.5 miles) is closed but not locked. At the junction with USFS Road #194, head north on the 2WD road, known to locals as Valley Road. This road parallels Idaho 75 through the south half of the Sawtooth Valley and meets up with Idaho 75 just before the turnoff to Fourth of July Creek, a major access point to the White Cloud Mountains. Enjoy the spectacular views of the Sawtooth Range, off to the west, as you pass through rolling terrain covered with sagebrush and lush grazing fields. The road is good, but it can be dusty and unpleasant for non-motorized use. After leaving the Sawtooth National Forest boundary (13.4 miles) the route traverses a mix of national forest and private land to join the Champion Creek road and end at Idaho 75 at 17.6 miles. Turn north onto the highway, pass the Fourth of July Creek road on the right and hook up with the Decker Flats Road #210, on the left side of Idaho 75 (17.9 miles). You'll cross the Salmon River, and then run parallel to Idaho 75 and follow along the base of Hell Roaring ridge. Keep right when the road splits and enter a big open area which provides outstanding vistas of the Sawtooth peaks. Stop to enjoy them and take photos or hike to the Salmon River for some good trout fishing. The road crosses a cattle guard and a bridge and leaves the open fields to again follow along the base of a forested ridge. At a dirt road junction, #210 goes left and winds uphill to a junction with an access road to a summer home area. Go straight at that junction and follow #210 as it drops to the Redfish Lake Road at 6,500 feet.

At Redfish Lake Road, the original Centennial West route followed an old stock driveway in the lower foothills of the Sawtooths over to Iron Creek. There is no trail tread on the ground, however, so we recommend several alternative routes:

Alternate 1 -- Alpine Way Trail (open to hikers, stock users) 13.7 miles: This is a single-track trail that wanders along the Sawtooth Wilderness Boundary from Redfish Lake area to Iron Creek. From the junction with #210 and Redfish Lake Road, cross the Redfish Lake Road and head to a parking area with Forest Service information. Cross the Redfish Creek bridge and take the trail to the left. This passes Little Redfish Lake, gradually climbs the ridge and joins Alpine Way Trail #528. Keep right at junctions to the Redfish Corals, Fishhook Creek and the Bench Lakes (about 1.5 miles), and continue up the open ridge on this well traveled, single track trail. Terrific views of spire-studded Heyburn Peak and Horstman Peak can be seen a few steps to the left in the open slopes. The trail then climbs steep through forest to its highest point (8,040 feet.) After crossing Goat Creek, turn right on the Iron Creek Trail #640 at about nine miles and 7,210 feet. Descend on the Iron Creek Trail to the trailhead and the Iron Creek Road. Proceed toward Stanley on the Iron Creek Road for about 2.7 miles.

Alternate 2 -- 6.7 miles: The shortest and quickest bypass is to head back to Idaho 75 on the Redfish Road, turn left and proceed to Stanley. Turn left at the junction of Idaho 21 and Idaho 75 and proceed west of Stanley to the marked turnoff for the Iron Creek Road, #619. Turn left onto the Iron Creek Road and follow it less than a half mile to the edge of the forest, to a two-track trail junction.

ron Cr. Road to Stanley Lake -- 7.3 miles on Stock Driveway Trail #102

Centennial East takes off from the Iron Creek Road on a two-track trail at the edge of an open and forested area. The two-track and single track trail is well marked with Idaho Centennial Trail and Idaho snowmobile signs. This multi-use trail passes through forest and meadows with grazing stock and offers some unusual and picturesque views of the northern Sawtooth peaks. Follow the two-track trail northwest past the Idaho DOT work center and gravel stockpile. Turn left on a graded dirt service road, then continue on a short single-track to Crooked Creek road

Roger Williams

If you have a chance, take a side hike from Stanley Lake to Observation Peak (9,151 feet) to get a bird's eye view of Mt. Regan, Merritt Peak, Williams Peak, Thompson Peak and Baron Peak, all over 10,000 feet.

USFS #693 (1.3 miles). Orange "Stock Driveway" signs mark a single-track trail on the right side of the road where it enters the forest. At the forest's west edge, cross the large open meadow diagonally and go uphill. Cross a small wooden bridge and continue northwest following yellow stock driveway and Centennial Trail signs. At Job Creek, cross the meadows keeping near a signpost to avoid the boggy areas. Yellow "Stock Driveway" signs help locate the route on the far side where the trail joins an unmaintained road, USFS #455. This passes some summer homes and descends a steep hill to join the Stanley Lake road, USFS #455. Go left toward the mountains past Stanley Lake to the Inlet Campsite (7.3 miles). Here, Centennial East joins the main Centennial Trail.

Historical and interpretive notes: The **Stanley Basin Stock Driveway** (Trail 102) was established in the early 1900s to provide a route to move sheep and cattle from grazing pastures in the Stanley Basin to Ketchum. Here, the livestock were shipped to market by rail or herded down the Wood River Valley to neighboring ranches. Grazing in the basin is still a common sight, but stock drives over Galena Summit have long since been replaced by stock trucks... **The historic Stanley Ranger Station,** located a mile up Pole Creek on USFS Road #197, is well worth a visit.

#9 Stanley Lake to Dagger Falls

South access: Stanley Lake
North access: Dagger Falls Campground
Distance: 18 miles
High point: 7,140 feet
Low point: 6,513 feet
Type of trail: Single-track trail, dirt road,
paved highway
Uses allowed: Hiking, stock users, mountain
bikes, motorcycles, and vehicles. Marsh
Creek is closed to motorized use and
mountain bikes.
Terrain: Fairly level meadows and forests
Access to water: Excellent
Overview map: Sawtooth National Recreation Area
Topo maps: Elk Meadows, Banner Summit, Cape Horn Lakes, Chinook Mountain

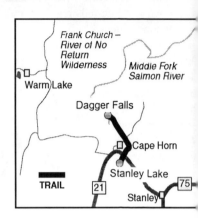

Directions to South Access: From Stanley, take Highway Idaho 21 west about six miles to the well-marked turnoff for Stanley Lake, USFS Road #455. Turn left and head to a junction with USFS Road #649. The Centennial Trail follows the road to the Elk Meadows Trail #629.

Directions to North Access: Take Idaho 21 to the Boundary Creek turnoff, about three miles east of Banner Summit, between Lowman and Stanley. Head north on the washboard-prone dirt road, USFS #082, to Bruce Meadows. Turn right on USFS #568 to Boundary Creek and Dagger Falls campgrounds. The Marsh Creek trail can be accessed from a bridge crossing the Middle Fork of the Salmon River at the campground.

Best Supply Points: Stanley.

Trail description: This route takes Centennial Trail travelers from Stanley Lake to Elk Creek Meadows, across the Stanley Basin, and then down Marsh Creek to Dagger Falls. It presents a very scenic tour of the headwaters of the nationally famous Middle Fork of the Salmon River. The Centennial Trail follows a series of high meadows in Stanley Basin and then descends on a gentle roll along Marsh Creek, a crystal clear tributary with good fishing. **To begin,** turn onto USFS Road #649 just short of Stanley Lake. The road climbs at a fairly steep grade for 1.5 mile to a dirt parking area on the left at the signed junction with the Elk Mountain Loop Trailhead (Trail #629). Proceed on Trail #629 to Elk Meadows. It's a rocky, single track trail through the woods. Mountain bikers will feel the bumpy trail shake up their insides. In three miles, the trail emerges into the lush Elk Meadows where elk can be seen grazing in the early morning and late evening soon after snowmelt.

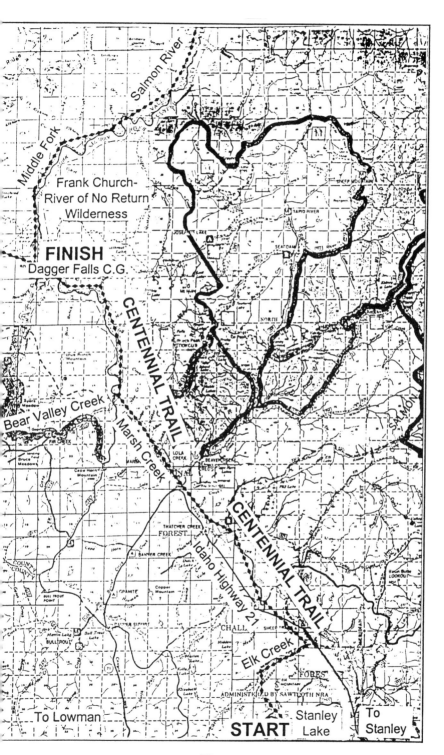

Salmon River

Middle Fork

Frank Church-
River of No Return
Wilderness

FINISH
Dagger Falls C.G.

CENTENNIAL TRAIL

Bear Valley Creek

Marsh Creek

CENTENNIAL TRAIL

FOREST

Idaho Highway 21

CHALL

Elk Creek

FORES

ADMINISTERED BY SAWTOOTH NRA

To Lowman

Stanley
START Lake

To
Stanley

Mark Lisk

Stanley Lake is a very popular car-camping, fishing, boating and hiking destination on the north end of the Sawtooths.

Later in the summer, the meadows are grazed by livestock. Watch for a junction with Trail #614 on the left side of the large meadow. A new trail has been constructed around the north side of Elk mountain to avoid fording Elk Creek. Go right at the junction with a two-track trail (5.0 miles) and cross a log bridge to a parking area on Elk Creek Road, USFS #614. Follow the road downhill just past a distinct road junction. Turn left onto the Stock Driveway (6.5 miles) which follows a two-track into the woods. Follow Centennial Trail and Idaho snowmobile signs about one-half mile to Meadow Creek and cross over to Sheep Trail Campsite on logs. If the creek is high follow it to the right and cross the creek on Idaho 21. A fairly good single-track trail follows snowmobile and Centennial Trail signs along the highway from Sheep Trail campsite to a gate on the highway at 7.6 miles. Exit at the gate and take Idaho 21 west (left) to Old Bear Valley Road, USFS #203, on the left side of the highway. Cross a cattle guard and continue on this excellent dirt road for 8.0 miles as it passes through Stanley Basin and Cape Horn Guard Station area. Early in the year, the panorama of the northern Sawtooth range is enhanced with an abundance of wildflowers in the meadows along Marsh Creek. Stay on the main road as you pass many small roads to the north and cross Kelly Creek and Asher Creek, two possible sources for replenishing drinking water. Continue past the turnoff for the Bradley Scout Camp, and then turn right onto USFS #083, which dead-ends at the Marsh Creek Campsite and trailhead. It is a delightful hike down the Marsh Creek single-track trail into the Frank Church-River of No Return Wilderness. Bring your fly rod

60

The Middle Fork of the Salmon River, upstream from Dagger Falls, flows gin-clear.

if you like to catch trout. All fish must be released. The Marsh Creek Trail descends on a slightly downhill grade all the way to Dagger Falls. The trail tread is mostly well-maintained with water bars. Five miles down Marsh Creek is a glory hole of sorts called the Big Hole, a giant pool where Bear Valley Creek meets Marsh Creek. This is a spot where salmon and steelhead rest on their journey to spawning grounds 850 miles from the sea, and today, it's a great trout fishing hole. Even if the fish aren't biting, you can still see them congregated in the dark recesses of the inky pool. From the Bear Valley confluence, it's seven miles to the Dagger Falls campground. Here you can enjoy watching the water crash through the gnarly series of waterfalls. Developed campsites are located by the falls and at Boundary Creek Campground, just next door, the gateway to the Middle Fork of the Salmon River.

Historical and interpretive notes: The **Stanley Basin Stock Driveway** (Trail #102) was established in the early 1900s to provide a route to move sheep and cattle from excellent grazing in the Sawtooth basin to Ketchum. Here they could be shipped to market by rail or herded down the Wood River Valley to neighboring ranches. Grazing in the Basin is still a common sight, but stock drives over Galena have long since been replaced by stock trucks. However, you may be lucky enough to meet a band of sheep or a herd of cattle along the Driveway, especially at the north end of the SNRA. A single herder with his horse and faithful dogs can keep several hundred sheep on the Driveway. If you should be lucky enough to witness this historic scene, be aware that herding dogs may attack your pet dog if they perceive it to be a threat. For this reason, it is best to keep your dog on a leash where any stock are grazing.

#10 Dagger Falls to Thunder Mountain

North access: Thunder Mountain, east of
Yellow Pine
South access: Dagger Falls or Boundary
Creek campground
Distance: 52.5 miles
High point: Thunder Mountain, 8,579 feet
Low point: Marble Creek Trail jct., 4,500
feet
Type of trail: All single-track
Uses allowed: Hiking, horseback, pack
stock.
Terrain: Well-traveled forest trail along the
Middle Fork of the Salmon River; rocky in

spots, with several washouts and blow-down. Marble Creek trail has downfall,
overgrowth and rocks.
Season: Late June to early October
Access to water: Excellent (be sure to purify)
Overview map: Frank Church-River of No Return Wilderness map, South half.
Topo maps: Big Soldier Mountain, Soldier Creek, Artillery Dome, Pungo Mountain, Norton Ridge, Safety Creek.

Directions to South Access: Take Idaho 21 to the Boundary Creek turnoff, about
three miles east of Banner Summit, between Lowman and Stanley. Head north on
the washboard-prone dirt road, USFS #082, to Bruce Meadows. Turn right on USFS
#568 to Boundary Creek and Dagger Falls campgrounds. It's best to camp at
Dagger Falls in mid-summer, because whitewater boaters cram into the Boundary
Creek campground, the launch site for Middle Fork river trips. Stock users should
park their rigs at a special parking area a mile or so above the Boundary Creek
Campground. The trail starts here.

Directions to North Access: Drive to Yellow Pine, via Cascade (best), Warm Lake
or McCall. It's a long curvy road to the mountain burb of Yellow Pine. Go east
from Yellow Pine on USFS #412 to Stibnite. The road changes to #375 over
Monumental Summit to the trailhead at Lookout Mountain Ridge campground.

Best resupply points: Stanley, Cascade or McCall. Yellow Pine has a few bars and
a cafe, but not much in the way of groceries. In a pinch, Warm Lake has a store.

Trail description: This section of the Centennial Trail is a dandy. It cruises through
the nationally renowned Middle Fork of the Salmon River canyon for about 30
miles, passes by several hot springs, and then it climbs out of the deep gorge on the
Marble Creek Trail, rising about 3,000-vertical feet over about 20 miles to Thunder
Mountain. The entire trail runs through fairly dense forest, with occasional open-

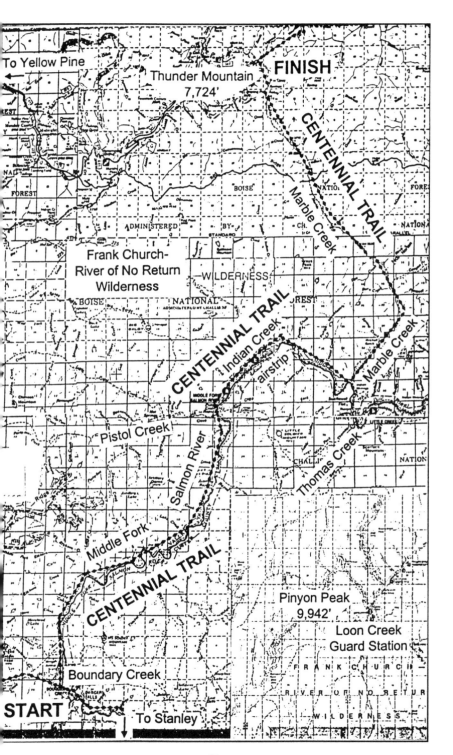

ings, rock scree slopes, downfall and washouts. Along the Middle Fork, the trail is in pretty good condition. "It's a highway," as one Forest Service ranger describes it. On Marble Creek, the trail gets progressively less traveled as you get 10 miles away from the Middle Fork. In this area, expect to encounter more obstacles and overbrush in that section. The trail runs along either the Middle Fork and its many tributaries, or along Marble Creek, so you can't run out of water. **To begin,** head down the Middle Fork Trail, on the left bank of the wild and scenic Middle Fork of the Salmon River. The trail winds under a thicket of lodgepole pine in the upper section (above 6,000 feet), and then as you travel down-canyon, more Douglas fir, ponderosa pine and aspen blend into the forest. On hot days, it's a shady walk on a dusty trail. In cooler, rainy conditions, the trail is shrouded with fog and muddy. Even if it's wet and rainy, remember to stop at several hot springs along the Middle Fork trail. The first hot spring is at Trail Flat Camp (river mile 4); the pool is adjacent to the rocky bank. There's a large hot spring at Sheepeater Hot Springs (river mile 12), directly adjacent to the main trail. A number of geothermal springs issue from cracks in the earth in a 200-yard-wide area. Ambitious backpackers might want to spend their first night next to the Sheepeater Springs. The river camp may be full of floaters, but there's plenty of space for camping (for either backpackers or stock users) near the springs, or at other campsites next to the Middle Fork, above and below the main Sheepeater river camp.

Continuing on, it's another scenic day of travel on a slight downhill grade from Sheepeater Hot Springs to Pistol Creek, a distance of about 10 miles. There is a gorgeous camp site and fishing hole next to the mouth of Pistol Creek. For backpackers, this would be a fine place to stop for the night. Even if Middle Fork boaters already occupy the main campsite, there is space on an upper bench behind the main camp. An outhouse, too. A deep fishing hole just below Pistol Creek Rapids, directly upstream of the campsite, contains big schools of cutthroat trout. In the glory days, this calm spot in the river was full of hundreds of chinook salmon, resting from their 800-mile journey home from the Pacific Ocean. From Pistol Creek, the trail heads by the Pistol Creek dude ranch, where a number of people have private cabins on a high bench above the river. There is an airstrip there, too. In two miles, you'll come to the Indian Creek airstrip and guard station. This is a huge bench above the river with public water. Indian Creek airstrip is a major resupply point or initial access point for Middle Fork floaters, both outfitters and private boaters. So be ready to hear a fair number of Cessnas taking off and landing in the morning. The airstrip can be useful for backcountry travelers in the early season: If Boundary Creek is smothered with snow in May, it's possible to fly into Indian Creek (4,250 elevation) to start backcountry trips from a lower elevation relatively free of snow.

Proceeding on, it's about 7.5 miles from Indian Creek to the Marble Creek junction. If you camped at Pistol Creek, you may want to spend the night in a small camp site at the mouth of Marble Creek. There is a much larger campsite upstream, which may be occupied by river floaters. The fishing here, next to the camp, can be wonderful in July, August and September. Proceeding up Marble Creek, on trail #222, you leave the Middle Fork canyon and head into some remote country. The trail should be clear of downfall for the first three miles to the Mitchell Ranch. Above that point, expect to encounter more downfall and rocks in the trail. The trail makes its first crossing upstream of the ranch. There will be many more crossings by the time you reach Thunder Mountain, an old mining zone. There will be more places to camp for backpackers and stock in the first 15 miles along Marble Creek, than the last five miles. After a long climb up Marble Creek, the trail reaches the top of Thunder Moun-

Roger Williams

The Middle Fork of the Salmon River canyon, near Marble Creek, is steep and spectacular.

ain, where there is a trailhead. This is a possible resupply point, the only access to a road until the Centennial Trail reaches the Magruder Road, on the north side of the Salmon River canyon.

Historical and interpretive notes: Nearly all 100 miles of the Middle Fork are protected inside the Frank Church-River of No Return Wilderness, at 2.3 million acres, the largest single wilderness area in the lower 48 states... **Encounters with whitewater boaters** will occur frequently during mid-summer along the Middle Fork. It's a very popular river as the premier wilderness river trip in America. If you're hungry or thirsty, you might ask boaters for a treat -- most of them carry plenty of beer... **Pistol Creek** is named after Pistol Rock, a granite landmark for backcountry explorers in the late 1800s and early 1900s. Many of the tributaries in Pistol Creek are named after guns -- inspired by the Sheepeater War in 1879 ... The Centennial Trail cuises through a portion of the **Idaho Batholith**, a thick mantle of white granite that underpins much of central Idaho. There are many intrusions of other sorts of minerals, too ... **Thunder Mountain** was the site of the last major gold rush in the West. Two brothers from Michigan, Ben and Lou Caswell, struck gold there in 1896 and mined $20,360 worth of gold in short stints over six years. They sold their claims for $100,000 to Col. William Dewey. In 1902, thousands of miners rushed to Thunder Mountain. Most of the gold was gone by 1909, ending the frontier mining era. Novelist Zane Grey visited the site and wrote a book titled *Thunder Mountain,* published in 1935. A modern gold mine was developed on Thunder Mountain in the late 1980s to tap the last of its riches.

#11 Thunder Mountain to Dry Saddle

North access: Dry Saddle, Magruder
Corridor Road
South access: Thunder Mountain, Lookout
Mountain Ridge C.G.
Distance: About 85 miles
High point: Lookout Mountain, 8,680 feet
Low point: Salmon River at Campbell's
Ferry, 2,330 feet
Type of trail: All single-track
Uses allowed: Hiking, horseback, pack stock.
Terrain: Well-traveled forest trail in the
Frank Church-River of No Return Wilder-
ness. Rocky in spots, with several washouts
and blow-down. Steep switchbacks in places.
Season: June to early October
Access to water: Excellent

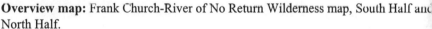

Overview map: Frank Church-River of No Return Wilderness map, South Half and
North Half.
Topo maps: Rainbow Peak, Monument, Acorn Butte, Wapiti Creek, Lodgepole
Creek, Meadow of Doubt, Sheepeater Mountain, Whitewater Ranch, Hida Point,
Sheep Hill, Sabe Mountain, Spread Creek Point.

Directions to South Access: Drive to Yellow Pine, via Cascade (best), Warm Lake
or McCall. Then, follow USFS #412 from Yellow Pine to Stibnite. The road
changes to #375 over Monumental Summit to the trailhead on Thunder Mountain.

Directions to North Access: Drive to Grangeville, south of Lewiston. Take Idaho
14 east of Grangeville and follow the signs for Elk City. Head for Dixie from Elk
City and then take the "Montana" Road, USFS Road #468 to Dry Saddle. It's a
long, bumpy and curvy gravel road for 31.3 miles. The signed trailhead is on the
south side of the road at Dry Saddle.

Best resupply points: Cascade, McCall, Grangeville or Elk City.

Trail description: This section of the Centennial Trail provides a magnificent tour
of a high-mountain forest environment in the dead-middle of the 2.3-million-acre
Frank Church-River of No Return Wilderness. Then the trail literally dives into the
main Salmon River canyon in a long series of switchbacks and crosses the river, the
traditional dividing point between north and south Idaho, at Campbell's Ferry. From
there, the Centennial Trail parallels the Salmon canyon for a short while before
climbing a very steep grade to Sheep Hill Lookout (elev. 8,405) and continuing on
in a high ridge to Dry Saddle and the Magruder Road. This is a huge section of wild
backcountry to travel through, 80-some miles. It should be a very arduous but

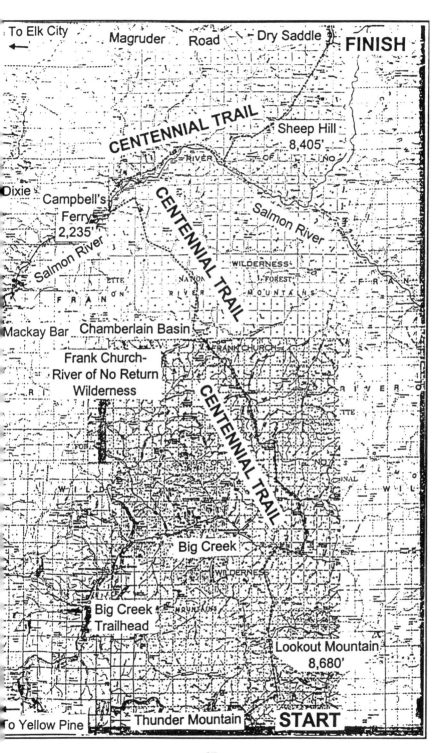

rewarding journey. **To begin,** hook up with Trail #061 at the Thunder Mountain Trailhead. The trail cruises along on ridgetops for about six miles to Lookout Mountain (elev. 8,680). From here, the trail heads north on a high ridge for about six miles until it descends into Big Creek, a major tributary of the Middle Fork of the Salmon River. Big Creek is a broad and open valley in this area, with many opportunities for camping. The Centennial Trail passes through little creek-side flats known as Hard Boil Bar, Over Easy Bar, and Soft Boil Bar. Enjoy the confluence of Coxey Creek at Coxey Hole on Big Creek, a premium fishing spot. Turn north on Coxey Creek on Trail #050 and head about five miles to Crescent Meadow, a good place to camp. Check with the Payette National Forest on camping restrictions in the meadow. Here, you'll cross the Crooked Creek Trail #002 and

Leo Hennessy

An old log cabin near Thunder Mountain stands as a testimonial to the last major gold rush in the West, from 1902-1909.

join Trail #010, going up the West Fork of Crooked Creek, and then bending north on Silver Creek. Just past Silver Creek Meadows, a junction with Trail #011 comes up at a ridgetop. Trail #010 continues into Whimstick Creek and the Root Ranch. Pick up Trail #011 and follow it for about five miles to Moose Meadows. This is a moist meadow area with several possibilities for campsites. By now, you've merged with Trail #002 from the Root Ranch and you're climbing from Moose Meadows to Moose Meadows Point, into the headwaters of Chamberlain Creek.

This is the upper gateway to Chamberlain Basin, a mile-high cool basin that's home to one of the largest elk herds in Idaho. You'll likely see moose here, too. It's about seven miles from Moose Meadows Point to the Chamberlain Basin Guard Station. There is a large two-story Forest Service lodge here with flush toilets, but it isn't open to the public. There also is a landing field (possible resupply point) and two private ranches nearby. The trail heads north from Chamberlain Basin, now Trail #001, along the West Fork of Chamberlain Creek for about eight miles to Dry Meadow, a large open meadow area with opportunities for camping. Same goes for Chamberlain Creek. The trail comes to a high-meadow divide at Wet Meadows (6,760 feet). Then it begins to descend along a gentle ridge to Trout Point (6,222 feet), the top of the Salmon River breaks, before taking a long plunge into the Salmon River canyon. There is a large pack bridge at Campbell's Ferry. It's about seven miles from Wet Meadows to the Campbell's Ferry bridge. Several colorful characters have lived at the Campbell's Ferry Ranch. Across the river, there is an historic homestead called the Jim Moore Place. It's actually a series of cabins and workshops on the wide Salmon River bar with many fruit trees. Black bear sightings here are common.

From Campbell's Ferry, the Centennial trail (now #096) proceeds upriver (east) along the north bank of the Salmon River for about 12 miles to Trail #576 at Rattlesnake Creek. You'll pass two Class 4 rapids, Elkhorn and Big Mallard, as you head up the trail. Whitewater Ranch, a private guest ranch, is about four miles upriver from Campbell's Ferry.

There is a dirt road that drops into Salmon River canyon here from Dixie, a possible access for resupply or for picking up new party members. In another three miles upriver, you'll pass a number of private cabins at Yellow Pine Bar. The Allison Ranch, a private guest ranch and airstrip (with a radio phone for emergencies) is 2.5 miles upriver. It's about four miles from Allison Ranch to the beginning of the ridge trail (#576) at Rattlesnake Creek. From here, it's a huge vertical climb to Dry Saddle, from 2,500 feet at the Salmon River

Stephen Stuebner

The Jim Moore Place, on the north bank of the Salmon River across from Campbell's Ferry, is on the National Register of Historic Places.

to 8,405 on the summit of Sheep Hill, a gain of nearly 6,000 vertical feet! (If you're only sampling a portion of the Centennial Trail, you may want to start at Dry Saddle and travel *downhill* to the Salmon River. Arrange for a jet boat pickup with a Riggins-based outfitter, and you can avoid having to climb back to Dry Saddle.) **Heading up the Salmon River grade,** the trail gains about 3,000 vertical feet in the first 4-5 miles. This is the steepest, lung-buster part of the climb. (Folks who climb this grade will have a full understanding of what it's like to climb the second-deepest gorge in the United States). After passing the shoulder of Crofoot Point (5,654 feet), the grade becomes more gradual. The main trail may be hard to discern from braided big game and stock paths. There is a series of many switchbacks between the head of the West Fork of Rattlesnake Creek and the final approach to Sheep Hill. Once you're on the high ridge, consider making camp at Sheep Spring Lake or the Lake Creek Lakes. It's less than eight miles from this area to Dry Saddle and the Magruder Road. Enjoy many spectacular views from this high vantage point, particularly the Bitterroot peaks to the northeast on the Idaho-Montana divide.

Historic and interpretive notes: Campbell's Ferry is named for William Campbell, an early settler in Chamberlain Basin, who operated a ferry service for miners across the Salmon River beginning in 1900. Campbell charged miners 50 cents to cross the river, cows $1... Campbell also helped build the Three-Blaze Trail, a more direct route for miners to reach Thunder Mountain.

69

#12 Dry Saddle to Wilderness Gateway

South access: Magruder Road, east of Elk City
North access: U.S. 12, Wilderness Gateway Campground
Distance: 105-110 miles
High point: Stanley Butte, 7,362 feet
Low point: Selway River at Three Links Creek, 1,930 feet
Type of trail: Mostly single-track, 4WD dirt road
Uses allowed: Hiking, horseback, pack stock (small section open to mountain biking, motorcycles and ATVs).

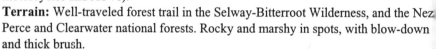

Terrain: Well-traveled forest trail in the Selway-Bitterroot Wilderness, and the Nez Perce and Clearwater national forests. Rocky and marshy in spots, with blow-down and thick brush.
Season: Late June to early October
Access to water: Excellent
Overview maps: Nez Perce National Forest, Selway-Bitterroot Wilderness.
Topo maps: Spread Creek Point, Sabe Mountain, Green Mountain, Three Prong Mountain, Wylies Peak, Moose Ridge, Shissler Peak, Mink Peak, Big Rock Mountain, Fish Lake, Fenn Mountain, Huckleberry Butte.

Directions to South Access: Drive to the Red River Ranger Station, via Elk City and Grangeville. Just south of Red River, turn left on USFS Road #468, the Magruder Corridor Road, also known as the "Montana Road" and the Nez Perce Trail. It's a 2WD washboard-prone dirt road that winds through the northcentral Idaho wilderness 113 miles to Darby, Mont. It's about 31.3 miles from here to Dry Saddle, and 24 miles to Poet Creek Campground. You can pick up the Centennial Trail at either one of these two points.

Directions to North Access: Drive east of Lewiston on U.S. 12 about 123.5 miles to Wilderness Gateway Campground.

Best resupply points: Grangeville or Lewiston. Elk City has several bars, cafes and supply stores that have basic groceries and fishing gear.

Caution: Carry a water purifier for treating water.

Trail description: This section of the Centennial Trail traverses a large section of the 1.2-million-acre Selway-Bitterroot Wilderness in a south-north direction, and the route parallels the national wild and scenic Selway River for 11 miles. Get ready for lots of up-and-down traveling through a wet forest environment. Sightings of

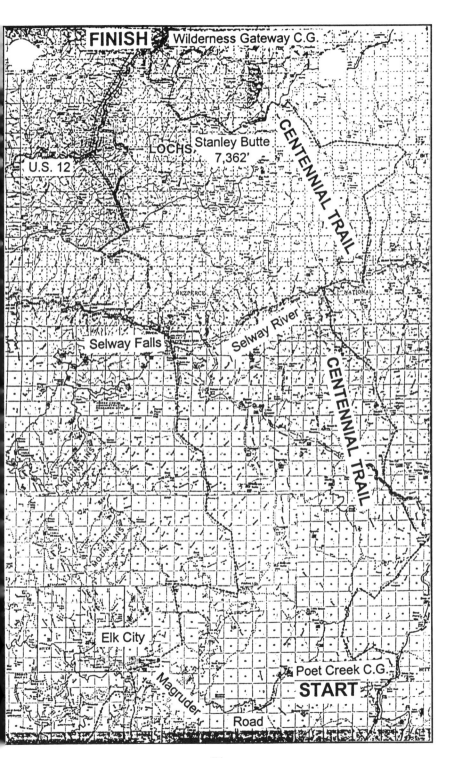

FINISH Wilderness Gateway C.G.

CENTENNIAL TRAIL

LOCHS Stanley Butte 7,362'

U.S. 12

Selway River

Selway Falls

CENTENNIAL TRAIL

Elk City

Magruder

Road

Poet Creek C.G.

START

moose and elk should be a cinch here in this remote, scenic and wild mountainous territory. The fly fishing (please catch and release the native cutthroat) is typically excellent on the Selway in July and August. **To begin,** we suggest starting this section of the Centennial Trail from the Poet Creek Campground. Volunteers ground-checked the "official" section of the trail from Dry Saddle to Burnt Knob lookout to the Bargamin Creek Trail, and the portion from Burnt Knob to Bargamin

Roger Williams

About 11 miles of the Centennial Trail run alongside the wild and scenic Selway River.

Creek is very rough and difficult to follow. It's a 4WD road from Dry Saddle to Burnt Knob. The trail from Poet Creek, however, is in fine condition from Bargamin Creek to the Green Mountain Road. Pick up the Bargamin Creek Trail #502 at Poet Creek Campground and follow the trail for about one mile. Watch for a single-track trail that peels off Bargamin Creek to the left

and heads uphill for the Green Mountain Road. This trail is open to mountain bikes, hikers and pack stock. Motorized vehicles could pick up the Green Mountain Road (USFS #285) from the Magruder Road. It's a relatively steep climb for about four miles to Green Mountain Road. At this junction, turn right and follow #285 for about 2.5 miles to a signed trailhead for Lynx Meadows and Warm Springs Bar, Trail #534. The trail drops directly off the ridge (6,800 feet) to Lynx Meadows (5,700 feet) and continues downhill to Warm Springs Bar (3,880 feet). About two miles after Lynx Meadows, the trail merges with a 4WD road, #285, which runs from Magruder Road to Running Creek and dead-ends. At Warm Springs Bar, pick up a single-track trail, #531, that heads up Patrol Ridge. It's all single-track wilderness trail now to Wilderness Gateway. The trail climbs at a very steep pace in the first several miles up Patrol Ridge to reach several peaks that exceed 6,500 feet on the Selway-Bitterroot Wilderness boundary. In about four miles, you'll come to a junction with Trail #530. Turn left and follow Trail #530 for about two miles. At the next junction, with Trail #529, bear left and follow #529 downhill into a high saddle at the headwaters of Tom Creek. Cross the creek, and follow the trail to a junction with Trail #562, which heads into Long Prairie Creek and the Selway-Bitterroot Wilderness. Enjoy the pretty meadows along Long Prairie Creek, a nice foreground to Box Car Mountain (7,589 feet). The trail descends along the creek at a very gentle pace for several miles. Good camping potential here. After you cross Goat Creek and its north fork, Trail #562 proceeds north and begins a gradual climb to a wooded saddle, the Goat Creek-Ditch Creek divide. Ignore junctions with Trails #526, #602 and #523, and stay with #562 as it heads north on an up-and-

72

down cruise along Moose Ridge for some 18 miles to the Selway River. The trail along Moose Ridge is delightful: It stays high, passing in and out of the trees and open slopes facing the awesome Bitterroot Range. You'll pass an elk hunting camp with spring water. Ignore a junction with Trail #547 as it comes in from the right just above Bitch Lake. Just above the lake, there is a great camp spot at the edge of the trees. The trail on Moose Ridge continues another four miles before it begins a big descent of 4,700 feet through trees and brush into the Selway River canyon. A nice view of the grassy meadows at Moose Creek landing strip appears before the final drop into the river bottom. Trail #562 crosses a pack bridge just upstream of Tony Point campsite and ends at Trail #4. At the Moose Creek junction, take a moment to check out the extensive tall-grass meadows and the historic ranger station. The series of parking spots for small aircraft and picnic tables make this sight look like the equivalent of a deluxe Cessna campground.

Proceeding on down the Selway River, follow Trail #4 on the river-right (north) side of the Selway River for the next 11 miles. If you're traveling this area in June or July, you may be able to watch kayakers and other whitewater boaters try to navigate a series of five Class 4-plus rapids below Moose Creek. It's known to floaters as "Moose Juice." The rapids, in sequence, are Double Drop, Ladle (the toughest), Little Niagara, Puzzle, No Slouch and Miranda Jane. The series of rapids ends just upstream of Cedar Flats campground, a gorgeous spot. At Three Links Creek, sadly, it's time to leave the Selway River and climb — again. Turn right on Trail #405 and follow it a short distance to the junction with Trail #606, and then follow #606, which heads directly up Sixty-Two Ridge. The trail on the ridge is bordered by heavy brush, and it can be hard to distinguish at times. The climb out of the Selway goes from 1,930 feet to 4,600 feet in less than two miles, and continues to climb past Bear Wallow Lookout (5,259), High Spring (6,512) and finally, a high point of 6,803 just short of Big Rock Mountain (7,103 feet). Peel left on Trail #693, which descends to a saddle and climbs again to a junction with Trail #423 under the shadow of Blacktail Butte. Turn right on #423, a very brushy trail that's difficult to follow, and descend into Lizard Creek and Rhoda Creek, a possible campsite. At the Rhoda Creek ford, turn left on Trail #620 and head up Rhoda Creek a short ways until the trail climbs a ridge that separates Rhoda Creek and Grotto Creek to lower Two Lakes, a beautiful camp spot. At the lower lake, pick up Trail #260 and then Trail #206 for the best route to Upper Two Lakes. Trail #218 has lots of downed trees and brush. Trail #206 strikes out on a major divide ridge between the Selway and Lochsa rivers, and the Nez Perce and Clearwater national forests. It continues uphill to Shasta Lake and Stanley Butte (7,362 feet). The trail skirts the shoulder of the butte, but it's worth climbing to the summit to check out an abandoned lookout and savor an excellent view of the Selway Crags. Pick up Trail #220, and drop into a delightful nest of lakes in Seven Lakes Basin. There are many potential camp spots here. Head northwest out of the lakes basin on the ridge spine and climb to Huckleberry Butte (6,701 feet). From here, it's a huge descent into the Lochsa River canyon at 2,101 feet.

#13 Dagger Falls to Caton Lake
(Centennial West)

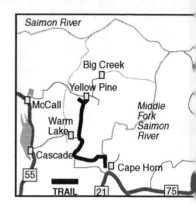

South access: Dagger Falls Campground
North access: South Fork Salmon River Road
Distance: About 40 miles
High point: Cox Creek Pass, 7,900 feet
Low point: Johnson Creek, 5,100 feet
Type of trail: Single-track, 4WD road, 2WD dirt road
Uses allowed: Hiking, horseback, mountain biking, motorcycles, and ATVs (in certain sections).
Terrain: Lush forest high-elevation terrain, rocky in places with blow-down.
Season: July to early October
Access to water: Excellent
Overview map: Boise National Forest
Topo maps: Chinook Mountain, Tyndall Meadows, Landmark, Log Mountain, Caton Lake

Directions to South Access: Take Idaho 21 to the Boundary Creek turnoff, about three miles east of Banner Summit, between Lowman and Stanley. Head north on the washboard-prone dirt road, USFS #082, over Fir Creek summit to Bruce Meadows. Turn right on USFS #568 to Boundary Creek and Dagger Falls campgrounds. Stock users should park their rigs at a special parking area a mile or so above the Boundary Creek Campground. The trail starts either from the stock parking area, or from the Boundary Creek guard station.

Directions to North Access: Hook up with the South Fork Salmon River Road (USFS #674) from Warm Lake or McCall, and drive to the well-marked Reed Ranch airstrip. Pick up Trail #290 and head about five miles to Eagle Rock. Watch for Trail #091 to the east of Eagle Rock and pick up the Centennial Trail at the junction of Trails #091 and #090.

Best resupply points: Stanley, Cascade or McCall. In a pinch, Yellow Pine has a few bars and a café, and a few basic supplies.

Caution: <u>Carry a water purifier for treating water.</u>

Trail description: This section of the Centennial Trail provides a west alternative route to proceed north on trails and roads that are mostly open to multiple-use. The first section from Dagger Falls to the Sulphur Creek divide is inside wilderness, so

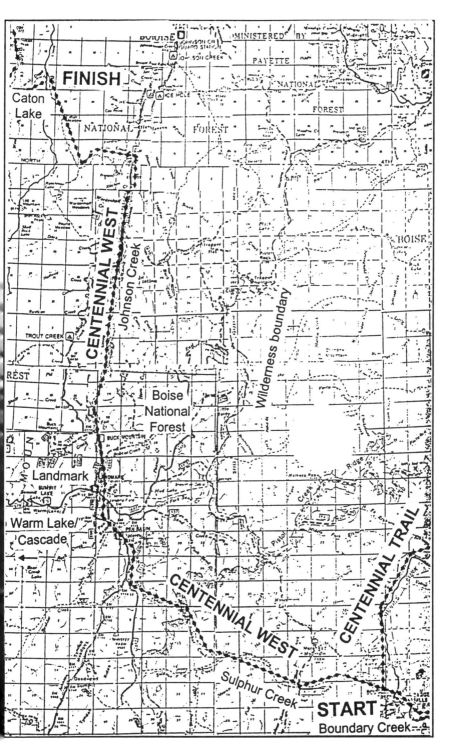

FINISH

Caton Lake

Johnson Creek

CENTENNIAL WEST

Boise National Forest

Landmark

Warm Lake/ Cascade

CENTENNIAL WEST

CENTENNIAL TRAIL

Wilderness boundary

Sulphur Creek

START

Boundary Creek

75

it is open only to hiking and horseback use. The route also provides excellent views of the rocky, timbered South Fork Salmon River country. **To begin,** head up the Middle Fork Trail #068 for less than a mile to a junction with the Sulphur Creek Trail #083. Turn left and head up Sulphur Creek. It's a beautiful, level cruise through the lower Sulphur Creek meadows and the Sulphur Creek Ranch and airstrip for the first six miles or so. At a junction with the North Fork of Sulphur Creek, split off from the main creek (still on Trail #083) and head up the North Fork to a saddle. If you got a late start, this junction might be a good spot to camp for the night. It's about four miles of steep climbing to the pass. The high divide at the pass marks the boundary of the Frank Church-River of No Return Wilderness. Once you drop into Whiskey Creek, you're in multiple-use land. The Whiskey Creek Trail descends about three miles into the upper Johnson Creek country, near Land-

Al Larson

It's quite rare to see a flying squirrel, but these critters do "fly" from one tree to the next in Idaho's forests.

mark. The Centennial West route hooks up with the Johnson Creek Road #579 and proceeds north by the Pen Basin Campground (nice spot for primitive car camping with outhouses) to Landmark, an historic sheep gathering area and airstrip. The little camping hub of Warm Lake is just over the hill to the west. At the Landmark junction, continue north on USFS Road #413 (the main 2WD dirt road to Yellow Pine). About three miles north of Landmark, peel off the road onto Burnt Log Trail #075 (the trailhead is north of Buck Mountain Campground). Burnt Log Trail jumps up on a ridge that parallels the road at a higher elevation and continues north for about 12 miles. ATVs should stay on the road; others can do so if they wish. The Centennial West route rejoins the Johnson Creek Road, just north of Halfway Station. Proceed north on the Johnson Creek Road for about four miles to the Cox Ranch turnoff. Watch for an access road to the Caton Lake trailhead that peels off to the left, right after the road crosses Johnson Creek. The jeep trail goes about a half-mile before it turns to single-track and heads for Caton Lake in earnest. It's a long, steep climb with many switchbacks out of the bottom of Johnson Creek (5,100 feet) to a pass at 7,900 feet at the head of Cox Creek and an upper fork of Caton Lake Creek. Once at the pass, however, it's a delightful cruise at high elevation for about three miles to Caton Meadow (7,200 feet) and then a short, steep descent into Caton Lake at 6,106 feet. Camping would be excellent at either Caton Meadow or Caton ake, depending on your preference. Be aware that mosquitoes may be present at the meadow.

Historical and interpretive notes: The **Sulphur Creek Ranch** is a dude ranch offering summer and fall accommodations. Elk hunting in Sulphur Creek is typically quite excellent ... **Landmark** got its name from early settlers who used a prominent granite rock in the area as a "landmark" marking the turn to Yellow Pine, Big Creek and Warm Lake. Today, it's a great car camping spot and recreation area. There is canoeing and fishing in Johnson Creek, and lots of trails in the area for multiple-use ... The **Cox Ranch** is a long-time dude ranch run by two generations of the Cox family. See *Idaho Mountains, Our Home -- The Life Story of Lafe and Emma Cox,* by Emma Cox (V.O. Ranch Books, 1997) for the whole story. The 160-acre ranch was homesteaded in 1909 by Alec Forstrum, who developed a strawberry patch and vegetable garden -- he even grew potatoes! Forstrum sold vegetables to miners at Thunder Mountain. Clark and Beulah Cox bought the ranch on Johnson Creek in 1927, and built up a successful fishing and hunting outfitting business in the surrounding countryside, including Chamberlain Basin and the Salmon River country. Lafe Cox, the son of Clark and Beulah, attended school in Yellow Pine, 10 miles away. He often traveled to school by dog sled. The Coxes charged $50 cents for a meal and $1 for a bed at the ranch in the early days. Johson Creek teemed with trout; the daily limit was 50 fish. Lafe Cox married a beautiful girl from Emmett, Emma R. Peterson, in 1939. They settled at the family's Mile High Ranch in Big Creek, where they had two daughters. Four years later, Lafe and Emma Cox took over the dude ranch on Johnson Creek, and Beulah and Clark Cox moved to warmer climes in Riggins. Lafe and Emma were very successful in the outfitting business, too, for many years. Emma Cox also drove a mail route and cooked delectible pies. They sold the dude ranch in 1974, and moved to the V.O. Ranch, 8.5 miles from Yellow Pine, which they still occupy today. They have a second home in Emmett.... Something to think about when you pass by the Cox Ranch on the way to Caton Lake, a place they used to visit frequently in the summer.

Fishing and Critters: The trout fishing can be quite good in Sulphur Creek, Johnson Creek and at Caton Lake. Watch for a wide diversity of birds and wildlife in this area. Just about every wildlife species known to frequent the wilds of the Northern Rockies, including endangered wolves, occupy this area. Watch for forest grouse, pileated woodpeckers, deer, elk, black bear, mountain lion, bobcat, mountain goats, bighorn sheep, redtail hawks, osprey, and golden eagles.

#14 Caton Lake to Wind River Bridge

(Centennial West)

South access: South Fork Salmon River Road
North access: Wind River Pack Bridge
Distance: About 58 miles
High point: Above Marshall Meadow, 8,080 feet
Low point: Wind River Pack Bridge, 1,998 feet
Type of trail: Single-track, 4WD road, 2WD dirt road
Uses allowed: Hiking, horseback, mountain biking, motorcycles, and ATVs (in certain sections).

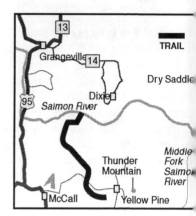

Terrain: Lush forest high-elevation terrain, rocky in places, some blow-down timber.
Season: July to early October
Access to water: Excellent
Overview map: Payette National Forest
Topo maps: Caton Lake, Teapot Mountain, Fitsum Peak, Enos Lake, Loon Lake, Victor Peak, Burgdorf, War Eagle Mountain, Johnson Butte, Carey Dome.

Directions to South Access: Hook up with the South Fork Salmon River Road (USFS #674) from Warm Lake or McCall, and drive to the well-marked Reed Ranch airstrip. Look for the trailhead for Trail #290 and head up the trail about five miles to Eagle Rock. Watch for Trail #091 to the east of Eagle Rock and pick up the Centennial Trail at the junction of Trails #091 and #090.

Directions to North Access: Drive to Riggins on U.S. 95. Turn east on the Salmon River Road #1614 and go about 28 miles to the Wind River Pack Bridge. Watch for a right-hand turnoff on USFS Road #318 that goes up the Carey Creek drainage. You can tie into the Centennial West route here.

Best resupply points: Cascade, McCall or Riggins. In a pinch, Yellow Pine has a few bars and a café, and a few basic supplies.

Caution: Carry a water purifier for treating water.

Trail description: This section of the Centennial Trail provides a west alternative route to proceed north on trails and roads that are mostly open to multiple-use. It parallels the main Centennial Trail, which courses south-north through the Frank Church-River of No Return Wilderness. Even though this section of Centennial

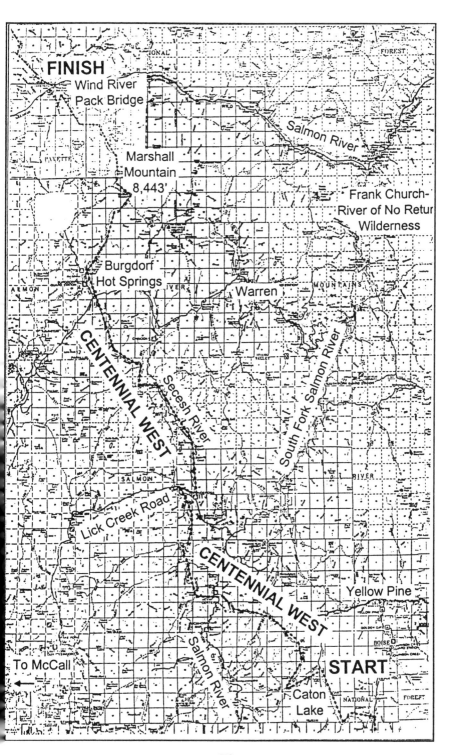

West isn't official wilderness, most of the areas will seem like it. You can look forward to traveling through some gorgeous lush forests in the Payette National Forest, and open ponderosa pine forests near Krassel and the south side of the Salmon River gorge. Most of this route features single-track forest trail that will be rocky and technical in sections for mountain bikes and motorcycles. Because most of the trail is single-track, ATVs will be limited to the southern-most section in the

Leo Hennessy

Mountain bikers cruise along Willow Basket Trail, a buffed single-track leading to Loon Lake.

old mining region around Marshall Mountain, and short sections near Lick Creek Road. **To begin,** head out of Caton Lake (6,108 feet) for a half-mile to the north, cross the outlet creek, and prepare for a sharp climb on an eroded trail with many switchbacks into the West Fork of Caton Creek, Sawpit Hill (7,576 feet) and Indian

Ridge, a skyline ridge that offers splendid views of the South Fork, the East Fork of the South Fork, and granite peaks. The trail on Indian Ridge rises to a high point of 7,820 on Indian Peak, and then it begins a gradual descent into the South Fork of the Salmon at Krassel Ranger Station. The Payette National Forest advises that the trail on Indian Ridge has been burned over and may be difficult to follow at times. It's about 15 miles from Caton Lake to Krassel (3,781 feet). If you're looking to camp sooner than Krassel, consider a nice meadow in upper Phoebe Creek, about 11 miles from Caton Lake. There is a trail that leads off the ridge to the meadow. Krassel Ranger Station has public water. Cross the South Fork on a pack bridge (slated for repair in the summer of 1998) and pick up the trail to Krassel Knob. It's a brisk climb to the knob. From here, turn right on Trail #088 and drop into the South Fork of Fitsum Creek. Turn left when you reach Fitsum Creek on Trail #087 for a short distance, to Trail #086, which jumps over a small ridge into the North Fork of Fitsum Creek. Prior to the bottom of North Fitsum Creek, you'll reach a junction with Trail #300, which climbs up Tie Creek to a ridge and then drops into the Lick Creek Road (access to McCall) and the Secesh River. Ponderosa Camp-ground, at the junction of Lick Creek and the Secesh, is a nice car-camping spot with water. The Centennial Trail heads north along the right bank of the Secesh, a good-sized stream that supports salmon and steelhead, for about 10 miles. It's an up-and-down trail along the river, but it's generally uphill all the way to the Loon

Creek junction. There are a number of small campsites along the river, but in some sections, the canyon is too steep next to the river. Expect to encounter overbrush and blow-down in this section of the Secesh River Trail. The next turn, at Loon Creek, is marked by a steel pack bridge and a sign. Turn left up Loon Creek and head for Loon Lake, a beautiful spot for camping or lunch. It's a two-mile climb from the Secesh to Loon Lake. Take a moment to enjoy the scenery.

Proceeding on, the Centennial Trail route heads for Willow Basket Creek and Ruby Meadows. Ignore Trail #081 that heads for Chinook Campground and head in a northwest direction along Willow Basket Creek. The forest is partially burned here, while the undergrowth is thick and lush. It's mostly level as the trail winds along Willow Basket Creek, and then it climbs to a little summit at 6,200 feet, and then descends again at a mostly level pace to Ruby Meadows, a series of wet, tall-grass meadows. You might need your bug juice here. About 5.5 miles from Loon Lake, the single-track trail on Ruby Meadows becomes a two-track trail. This trail is being turned into a wide single-track for ATVs, but 4WD vehicles will be prohibited. It's about 4.5 miles from this junction to the Burgdorf-Warren road. The Ruby Meadows jeep trail ends within sight of the turnoff to Burgdorf. The Centennial Trail route heads directly across the main highway and follows USFS Road #246 to Burgdorf Hot Springs and Burgdorf

Roger Williams

Moose thrive in lush habitat in the Payette National Forest.

Campground. Take some time to enjoy the hot springs. It costs a few dollars to soak. Bathing suits are required during daylight hours. Cabins are available for rent. The Centennial Trail route leaves the 2WD dirt road at Burgdorf Hot Springs and climbs toward Crystal Mountain, which is literally a mountain of quartz and crystal. About two miles up the road, Centennial West peels off to the left on Trail #140, heading northeast for Marshall Meadow and the Kimberly Mine. This section of the trail follows a high ridgeline and climbs to the highest point of this trail segment at 8,080 feet, directly above Marshall Meadow. It's about five miles from the Crystal Mountain area to the high ridge above Marshall Meadow. There are several possibilities for camping on the high ridge, or by small high mountain lakes below. Just above Marshall Meadow, Trail #140 meets a 4WD road, #318, which traverses the high ridge and skirts a series of old gold mines, the Mount Marshall Mine, Kimberly Mine, Leadville Mine, Golden Anchor Mine and Sherman Howe Mine. It's a huge seven-mile descent from the mines into the Salmon River canyon, Carey Creek and the Wind River Pack Bridge, 6,200 feet below.

#15 Wind River Bridge to Selway Falls

(Centennial West)

South access: Wind River Pack Bridge, 20 miles east of Riggins

North access: Selway Falls, USFS Road #223

Distance: 110 miles

High point: 7,600 feet, near Umbrella Butte

Low point: Salmon River, 1,985 feet

Type of trail: Single-track forest trail, 4WD road, 2WD dirt road

Uses allowed: Most areas open and accessible to mountain bikes and motorcycles, some portions open to ATVs, all to hikers and equestrians.

Terrain: Rocky, steep slopes rising out of the Salmon River canyon, giving way to densely forested, rocky terrain around the perimeter of the Gospel Hump Wilderness. Expect to encounter heavy overbrush and downed timber in places.

Season: Late June to early October

Access to water: Spotty on ridge trails and roads; good along streams.

Overview map: Nez Perce National Forest

Topo maps: Carey Dome, Hanover Mountain, Florence, Dairy Mountain, Sawyer Ridge, Sourdough Peak, North Pole, Orogrande, Moose Butte, Elk City, Black Hawk Mountain, Anderson Butte, Selway Falls.

Directions to South Access: Take U.S. Highway 95 to Riggins. At the southern edge of town, watch for a sign and a bridge leading to the Salmon River Road. Drive across the bridge and follow the improved road along the Salmon River to the Carey Creek boat-access site and the Wind River Pack Bridge, about 23.5 miles from Riggins. There is ample parking and restrooms here. Proceed across the bridge and hook up with the trail on the north bank of the Salmon River.

Directions to North Access: Drive on U.S. 12 east to Lowell, about 98 miles east of Lewiston. Turn right on USFS Road #223 and follow it about 18.5 miles to Selway Falls, a marked point of interest. Turn south across the Selway River bridge on USFS Road #443/290 and travel 2.1 miles to Slims Camp and Meadow Creek Trail #726, the Centennial West alternative route.

Best resupply points: McCall, Riggins, Grangeville or Kooskia. There is an RV campground, cafe and small store in Lowell.

Trail description: This section of the Centennial West route covers a huge swatch of country. Climbing out of the Salmon River canyon, the route follows many ridgelines around the perimeter of the Gospel-Hump Wilderness, through Florence,

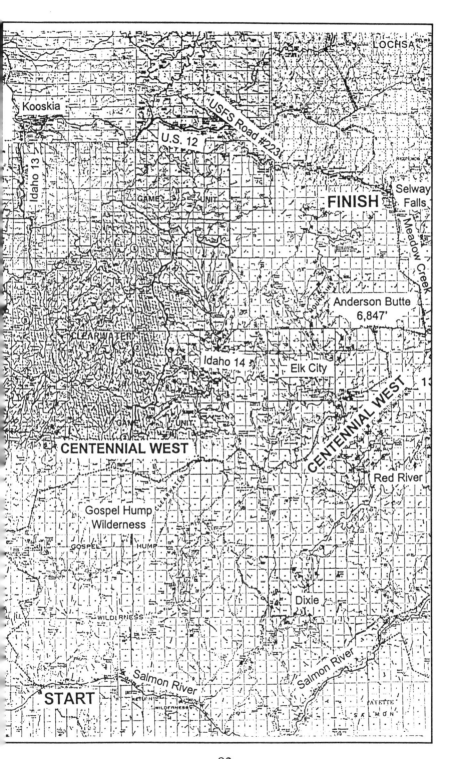

LOCHSA

Kooskia

USFS Road #223

U.S. 12

Idaho 13

GAME UNIT

FINISH

Selway Falls

Meadow Creek

Anderson Butte
6,847'

CLEARWATER

Idaho 14

Elk City

CENTENNIAL WEST

GAME UNIT

CENTENNIAL WEST

Red River

Gospel Hump
Wilderness

GOSPEL HUMP

Dixie

WILDERNESS

Salmon River

Salmon River

START

PAYETTE

SALMON

83

Orogrande and other historic dredge-mining areas near Elk City, and then after more ridge-walks, it descends into lovely Meadow Creek to Selway Falls. Anyone attempting this route in its entirety should reserve a major block of time, as much as two weeks, to cover the full 110 miles. Motorized trail users, of course, will be able to complete the trip faster than that. Please be aware that small portions of the route

Jeff Cook

Jeff Cook receives a visit from a friendly mule deer along the Centennial West trail.

and the Gospel Hump Wilderness are not open to motorcycles. In areas of conflict, we provide alternative trails or roads where possible. **To begin,** head across the Wind River Pack Bridge and bend to the left on a single-track (recently reconstructed and improved) trail #88 toward the Bullion Mine. This section of the trail is open to hikers, equestrians, mountain bikes and motorcycles. The trail rises at a steep grade and reaches the Bullion Mine in 1.5 miles, 2,000 feet above the river (whew!) The Bullion was one of many gold mines that were developed beginning in 1864 in the Florence Basin. Pick up a two-track trail heading north from the mine about 2.5 miles to a four-way junction with several logging roads. Turn right and follow USFS Road

#394 on a high ridge above Florence for about three miles. Hikers and equestrians should turn right at the junction with USFS Road #9922 and follow it about two miles until it dissolves into a single track trail, #332. This trail is open to hikers and stock users only; it follows the wilderness boundary for the next 10 miles on a high ridge. At the junction of USFS Roads #394/643B and Trail #88, motorcycles and mountain bikes should follow #643B, a 4WD route, to New Florence and continue, following old jeep trails, wagon roads and trails. Most of these roads were built to transport miners in the 1800s; the route was known as the Warren-Milner Military Access Road, servicing Grangeville, Warren and Burgdorf. In the future, this route will be labeled as Trail #88. Existing maps show the trails as #303, #338, #302, road #9307 and #310, leading to a junction with the stock/hiking trail coming out of the Gospel Hump Wilderness near Rocky Bluff Campground. Head north and follow the Forest Service dirt road outside the wilderness boundary to the junction with the road to Square Mountain Viewpont and Gospel Lake. Turn left at the junction and follow USFS #444A to Sawyer Ridge Point (7,303 feet). At the top of the mountain, the road turns into Sawyer Ridge Trail #328. Follow that for a mile. Then, Centennial West splits in two: Motorized users should proceed north on Trail #328 to Marble Point, American Creek, Buck Meadows and USFS Road #1862.

proceed on the 4WD dirt road to State Highway 14. Motorized users should travel on ID 14 for about 12 miles, past Fall Creek, to a junction with USFS Road #212 on Buckhorn Creek. Head south on #212, a steep 4WD mining road, for 2.4 miles to USFS Road #1894. Follow #1894 2.6 miles to the Sourdough-Santiam Road #492 and head east two miles to Summit Flats to join the original Centennial West route. Hikers and stock users can avoid this detour by taking a 90-degree right-hand turn on Trail #431, north of Sawyer Ridge, and drop into Johns Creek. The Forest Service warns this trail is chock- full of blow-down from major wind storms. About 2.5 miles from the Trail #431 junction, the trail switchbacks many times into the bottom of Johns Creek, a possible small camping spot. After you cross Johns Creek, the trail rises very steeply out of the canyon to a forested ridge heading for Sourdough Peak Lookout (6,800 feet). Route-finding may be difficult since the trail has very light use. At Sourdough Lookout, the trail turns into a jeep trail. Continue on the 4WD road, #492, and ignore several trails and roads that peel off to the left of the road in the first mile. About 1.5 miles from the lookout, you'll come to a junction with the main Santiam-Sourdough road and a primitive two-track, Trail #881, heading for 20-Mile Butte. Proceed to 20-Mile Butte. There are two excellent high lakes next to the butte for camping. The jeep trail continues to follow the wilderness boundary on a finger-ridge descent into the bottom of Williams Creek. Centennial West heads up Trail #802 along the ridge about five miles to a junction with USFS Road #478 and Summit Flat. The trail here is accessible again to mountain bikes, motorcycles and ATVs. It's a gravity ride from Summit Flat (6,075 feet) over a few knobs into the bottom of Crooked River and Fivemile Campground, less than a mile from the historic town of Orogrande. Dredge tailings are visible reminders of the gold-mining activity here.

Centennial West continues from the bottom of Crooked River on USFS Road #9836 and Trail #821, climbing up on a ridge and heading for Porters Mountain. It's about seven miles of climbing on the major dirt road to a junction with forest trail #820 to Porters Mountain. The Nez Perce National Forest does not recommend this trail for motorcycles. On top of Porters Mountain (6,411 feet), Centennial West follows forest trail #508 on a high ridge above Red River for about five miles into the bottom of Red River, where more dredge-mining is visible. There is a developed campground here called French Gulch. Proceeding on, head north on USFS Road #9822 for about three curvy miles to forest trail #833 heading for Blue Ribbon Mountain. Turn right and head for Blue Ribbon, a steep climb over two miles from the bottom Red River. Follow the jeep trail to the east of Blue Ribbon Mine toward the old Altemont Mine. Then turn left on a pack trail dropping into Horse Creek for about four miles. Watch for blow-down in this section. The trail intersects the road again, and then forest trail #505, heading along a major divide ridge to Anderson Butte. Here, motorized users and mountain bikes should follow the Anderson Butte National Recreation Trail #830 about eight miles to USFS Road #443, which eventually drops into the Selway Falls area. Hikers and stock users should take Trail #809 along Sheep Drive Ridge to Meadow Creek, and follow Meadow Creek, a proposed wilderness area, about 15 miles to Slims Campground.

#16 Selway Falls-Wilderness Gateway
(Centennial West)

South access: Selway Falls, USFS Road #223

North access: Wilderness Gateway Campground, U.S. 12

Distance: About 34 miles

High point: Roundtop Mountain, 6,807 feet

Low point: Glover Campground, 1,650 feet

Type of trail: 2WD dirt road, single-track, bushwack

Uses allowed: Hiking, horseback, mountain biking, motorcycles, and ATVs (in certain sections).

Terrain: Lush forest high-elevation terrain, rocky in places, some blow-down.

Season: Late June to early October

Access to water: Spotty after leaving the Selway River

Overview map: Nez Perce National Forest, Clearwater National Forest

Topo maps: Selway Falls, Chimney Peak, Coolwater Mountain, McLendon Butte, Huckleberry Butte.

Directions to South Access: Drive about 98 miles east of Lewiston to Lowell on U.S. Highway 12. Turn right on the Selway River Road (USFS #223) about 18.5 miles to the Selway Falls cabin and trail information. Pick up the Centennial Trail at the falls.

Directions to North Access: Drive about 123.5 miles east of Lewiston on U.S. Highway 12 to the well-marked turnoff for Wilderness Gateway Campground.

Best resupply points: Lewiston, Grangeville, Orofino, Kooskia. In a pinch, Lowell has a café, small store, RV park and motels.

Caution: Carry a water purifier for treating water.

Trail description: Please be aware that this section of Centennial West does not provide a multiple-use alternative route for the full section of the route. After the route reaches Glover Saddle, the trail proceeds to Fire Creek Point and disappears. Therefore, the only way down from Fire Creek Point is to bushwhack down a steep ridge to Split Creek Bridge, or take alternative trails. We suggest that hikers and stock users should go from Glover Saddle into the Selway-Bitterroot Wilderness and hook up with Trail #133 over Flea Ridge and Split Creek Point to reach the Split Creek Bridge. Multiple-use trail users should consider staying on Coolwater Ridge after passing Round Top Mountain and dropping into the Lochsa via Trail

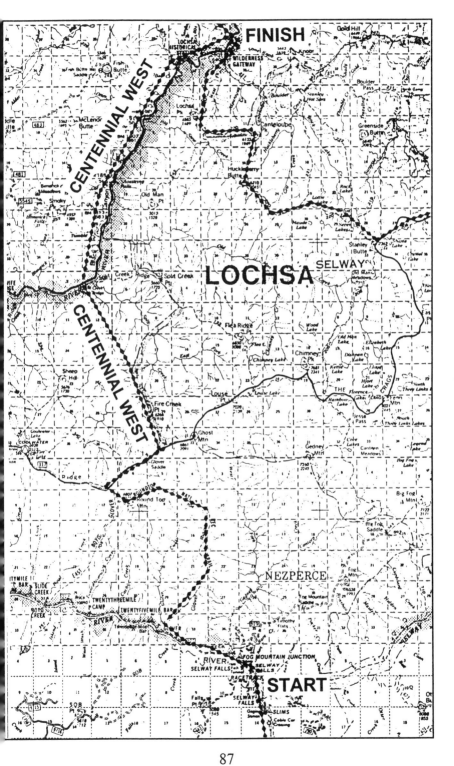

#317, a 4WD jeep road that follows Coolwater Ridge. **To begin,** head northwest on the Selway River Road #223 from Selway Falls for about 3.5 miles to Glover Campground. Here, Centennial West picks up the Round Top National Recreation Trail #704 on the east side of Glover Creek on the Selway Road. The trail climbs a ridge spine on a very steep grade. The trail is open to hikers, stock users, mountain bikes and motorcycles. In the first mile or so, the trail climbs from 1,650 feet at Glover Camp-ground to 3,827 feet, a vertical rise of nearly 2,200 feet! That kind of climb will cause most mountain bikers to wilt, leaving this section of trail most appropriate for hikers, stock users and motorcyclists.

Mark Lisk

Selway Falls drops 40 feet amidst boulders and foam. Two sections of Centennial West begin and end at the falls.

The climb contin-ues, albeit at a more reasonable rate, on Glover Ridge. It's 12.2 miles from the campground to Round Top Mountain (6,807 feet). At Round Top, the single-track meets a jeep trail, Coolwater Ridge Trail #317. Proceed one mile northwest of Round Top Mountain to a three-way junction. From here, wilderness travelers can peel off toward Glover Saddle and the Selway-Bitterroot Wilderness. Multiple-use travelers should proceed on #317 to Coolwater Lookout (6,929 feet), which has fetching views of Coolwater Lake, and goes on to Andy's Hump (6,470 feet) before it drops back to the Selway River, just short of Lowell. Depending on your prefer-ence, it also would be possible to do a shorter loop from Round Top Mountain and drop down the Boyd Creek Trail back into the Selway River at Boyd Creek Camp-ground. From Coolwater Ridge, hikers and stock users could consider several single-track trails that drop into the Lochsa Valley, but you'll have to cross the Lochsa River to reach the highway, an impossible feat at high water (unless you can get a raft to ferry you across. Regardless of which way you descend from Coolwater Ridge, the final reach of this section of Centennial West cruises along the north side of U.S. 12 and the Lochsa River, from Split Creek Bridge to Wilderness Gateway Campground. This section of Centennial West is maintained each year as a National Trails Day project.

From Glover Saddle, the best alternative route heads into the Selway-Bitterroot Wilderness by Ghost Mountain and follows a skyline route over Louse Point (7,020 feet) and Louse Lake, where a trail junction appears. Turn left and head north on Trail #133 into a lovely cluster of high lakes within view of Chimney Peak (7,681 feet), Fenn Mountain (8,021 feet) and the impressive Selway Crags – giant fins of granite that jutt higher than any other peaks in the western side of the 1.2-million-acre wilderness. Camping at either Chimney Lake or Flea Lake would be an excellent choice. From Flea Ridge Point, the trail descends quite rapidly toward the Lochsa River, passing by Split Creek Point before it drops into Split Creek drainage and follows many switchbacks into the bottom of the Lochsa canyon. It's an interesting contrast from the dry brushy slopes of the ridge and the lush, fern-covered bottom of the canyon.

Historical and interpretive notes: The **Roundtop National Recreation Trail** was developed to provide a loop trail for recreationists and give folks a vast view of the Selway River canyon ... **The Selway River** is a national wild and scenic river. The name comes from **Thomas Selway**, a sheep rancher from Montana who ran large bands of sheep in the wilderness in the 1890s and early 1900s. Legend has it that Selway is a Nez Perce word for "smooth water," but of course, the rapid-choked Selway River is anything but smooth through most of its course. Uncommonly pure, the Selway winds through the heart of the Selway-Bitterroot Wilderness from Paradise to Selway Falls. Tight regulations only allow one party to launch per day on the 50-mile wilderness whitewater journey ... **A bounty of car camping** locations are available all along the Selway River between Lowell and Selway Falls, and along the Lochsa River as well. The campsites get filled pretty fast on summer weekends, however ... **Coolwater Ridge** is an excellent spot for feeding horses due to its many high meadows. The Nez Perce used to feed their Appaloosas on the ridge, and later, the Forest Service grazed pack stock there.

Fish and Critters: The trout fishing can be excellent on the Selway River. The fishing is decent in the high lakes between Louse Point and Flea Ridge Point. Watch for a wide diversity of birds and wildlife in this area, especially moose, elk, black bear, mountain goats and deer.

#17 Wilderness Gateway to Kelly Forks

South access: U.S. 12, Wilderness Gateway Campground
North access: Kelly Forks via Kelly Creek Road #255, or via Hoodoo Pass and Superior, Mont.
Distance: About 45 miles
High point: Lookout Peak, 6,876 feet
Low point: Lochsa River, 2,100 feet
Type of trail: Single-track forest trail, 4WD road
Uses allowed: Hiking, horseback, small portions open to mountain bikes, motorcycles and ATVs
Terrain: Well-traveled forest and ridge-top

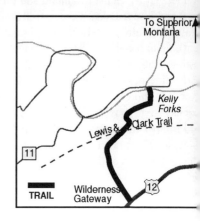

trail in the Clearwater National Forest. Rocky in spots, with several washouts, and heavy brush. Steep switchbacks in places.
Season: Late June to early October
Access to water: Good along streams; spotty along dry ridges.
Overview map: Clearwater National Forest
Topo maps: Huckleberry Butte, Liz Butte, Cook Mountain, Lookout Peak, Scurvy Mountain, Gorman Hill

Directions to South Access: Take U.S. 12 to well-marked Wilderness Gateway Campground. The trailhead for Sherman Creek is across the highway from the campground on the north bank of the Lochsa River.

Directions to North Access: Drive to the Kelly Forks Guard Station via Hoodoo Pass and Superior, Mont., or via Pierce, north of Kooskia, via USFS Roads #250 and #255 -- 40-plus miles of dirt road.

Best resupply points: Lewiston, Orofino, Kamiah, Kooskia or Superior, Mont. In a pinch, Lowell has some groceries and a cafe.

Trail description: Get ready for some big-time climbing, lots of big trees, and a slice of history on this section of the Centennial Trail. It's nearly 4,000 feet of vertical gain to ascend the north side of the Lochsa River canyon to Liz Butte and the top of the Lochsa Face. Then the trail plunges nearly 3,000 feet into Weitas Creek, before climbing up to Windy Ridge for a long, impressive skyline ridgewalk before dropping again into Kelly Creek canyon. **To begin,** head up Sherman Creek trail #203. It's a seven-mile, steep climb through an old burn to No-See-Um Meadows and the Lewis and Clark Trail, USFS Road #500. Expect to encounter overhanging brush in the first few miles. About five miles up, the trail becomes rutted and eroded for a time. In the last mile, the trail levels out a bit as it ap-

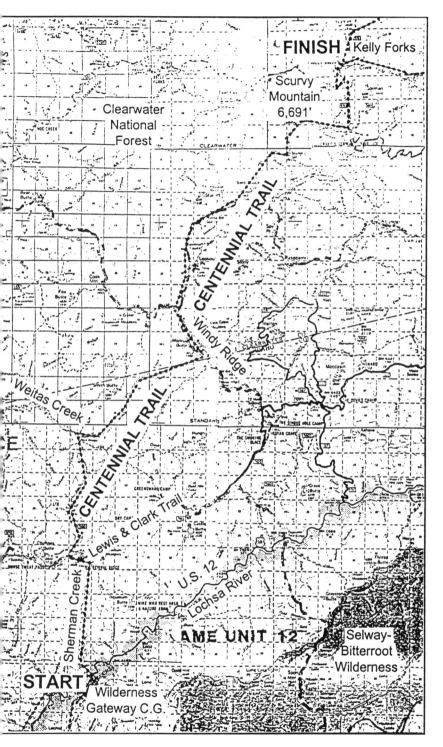

Roger Williams

The tranquil Kelly Creek canyon.

proaches No-See-Um Meadows and the #500 road Off to the west, you'll see Sherman Peak (6,658 feet) and Spirit of Revival Ridge. Sherman Peak was the spot from which Lewis and Clark first spotted a way out of the thick forest that had been a nightmare to cross, the most difficult part of their journey Take a sidetrip to Sherman Peak if you have the time. There are plenty of camping spots in the No-See-Um Meadows area, and in some high meadows on the way to Liz Butte. Continuing on, turn west on the #500 road and stay on the single-lane dirt road for one mile to a junction with a 4WD road to Liz Butte Lookout. Head north about two miles to the lookout. Pick up a single-track trail at the summit and enjoy a fast descent into the forks of Weitas Creek and Windy Creek. This would be another excellent place to camp.

Proceeding on, the Centennial Trail climbs 3,000 feet up Windy Creek over 7-plus miles to Windy Ridge and Monroe Butte (6,522 feet). It's possible to scramble down to Monroe Lake from the ridge if you're ready to make camp, or to dip a line The Windy Ridge Trail #164 climbs at a moderate pace from the Monroe Butte are to the back shoulder of Lookout Peak (6,876 feet). Consider dumping your pack fo a short hike to the top of Lookout Peak. Continuing north, Lookout Lake is too small for good fishing. The ridge trail kind of yo-yos as it heads north on this high divide between Cayuse Creek and Kelly Creek, both impressive and deep canyons The trail hits a high point at Switchback Hill, drops to Scurvy Saddle and then climbs again to a knob overlooking Scurvy Lake. It's all downhill now, to a three-way road junction on East Saddle, and onward down Clayton Creek to Kelly Forks Guard Station.

Historical and interpretive notes: The route followed by **Lewis and Clark** from Lolo Pass to the Weippe Prairie is now a single-lane dirt road called the Lolo

The view from the Lewis and Clark Trail offers big vistas of the snow-capped Selway Crags, top, in the Clearwater National Forest.

Motorway, or the "500 Road," named for USFS Road #500. Lewis and Clark encountered more trouble (harsh, snowy weather in September, and lack of game in 1804) as they tried to pass through the north side of the Lochsa River canyon than anywhere else on their entire route. When the Corps of Discovery came back through in the spring of 1806, they tried to push into deep snow and were forced to turn back until the snow melted ... **A U.S. Army construction crew** that built a military road over Lolo Pass named Sherman Peak for Gen. William T. Sherman in 1868 ... **Windy Ridge** was named as such for obvious reasons, being a high, exposed ridge spine in the Clearwater National Forest ... **Scurvy Mountain, Scurvy Creek and Scurvy Lake** were named for George Gorman and Clayton Shoecraft, who lived in a small cabin in the Cayuse Creek area in the fall of 1907. They killed big game for meat and ran a trap line on Cayuse Creek. The men's diaries indicated failing health during the winter, and by the spring, they had died from scurvy. Their graves are located on Scurvy Mountain.

Fish and critters: Kelly Creek is a favorite spot for fly fishers because the cutthroat trout fishing can be excellent. It may be worth dipping a line in Weitas Creek, too. Please check with Fish and Game on catch-and-release regulations.

#18 Kelly Cr. G.S.-Hoodoo Pass
(Centennial Trail and Centennial West)

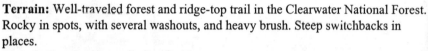

South access: Kelly Creek Road #255
North access: Hoodoo Pass via Superior, Mont.
Distance: 28-35 miles
High point: 7,256 feet near Dalton Lake
Low point: 3,200 feet, Kelly Forks
Type of trail: Single track forest trail, 4WD road
Uses allowed: Main Centennial Trail: Hiking and horseback. Centennial West: Most open to mountain bikes and motorcycles; some to ATVs.
Terrain: Well-traveled forest and ridge-top trail in the Clearwater National Forest. Rocky in spots, with several washouts, and heavy brush. Steep switchbacks in places.
Season: Late June to early October
Access to water: Good along streams; spotty along dry ridges.
Overview map: Clearwater National Forest
Topo maps: Huckleberry Butte, Liz Butte, Cook Mountain, Lookout Peak, Scurvy Mountain, Gorman Hill, Toboggan Ridge, Bruin Hill, Straight Peak and Hoodoo Pass.

Directions to South Access: Drive to the Kelly Creek Guard Station via Hoodoo Pass and Montana state route 257 from Superior, Mont., or via Pierce, north of Kooskia, via USFS Road #250 and #255 — 40-plus miles of dirt road.

Directions to North Access: Drive to Hoodoo Pass via Montana Highway 257 from Superior, Mont., or the Kelly Creek Road #255 via Pierce.

Best resupply points: Lewiston, Orofino, Kamiah, Kooskia or Superior, Mont.

Trail description for the main Centennial Trail through the Kelly Creek Roadless Area to Hoodoo Pass: This section of the Centennial Trail is an angler's special, following Kelly Creek, a blue-ribbon trout stream, for a good 10 miles before you climb up Hanson Ridge to Bruin Hill (6,504 feet) and then follow Bruin Ridge to Fish Lake and the Idaho-Montana Divide. About two-thirds of the route is at high elevations and offers spectacular vistas into both Idaho and Montana. Spots with magnificent views are available on the ridges for lunch and a nap but access to water requires giving away considerable elevation. In 1997 the trail between Fish Lake and Bruin Hill was cleared and reworked by the Forest Service. The Hanson

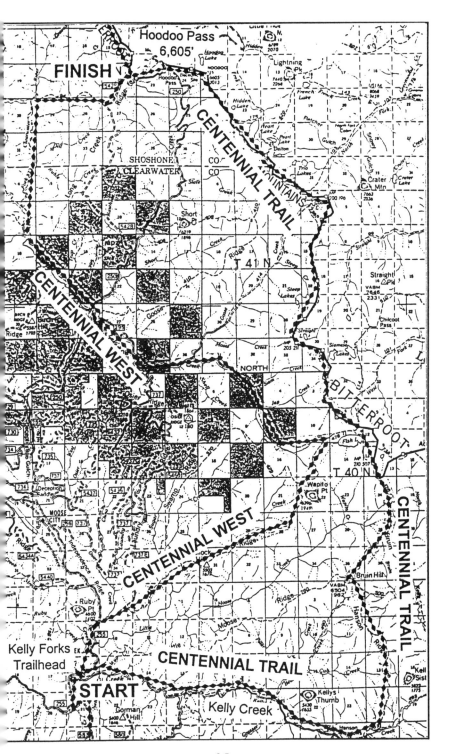

Ridge trail dropping into Hanson Meadows has lots of brush, typical of the north Idaho forest understory. **To begin,** follow Trail #567 out of Kelly Forks and head up Kelly Creek for about 10 miles to the Hanson Ridge Trail. An alternate choice between Bruin Hill and Kelly Creek is the easier Bear Creek Trail #490, which hits Kelly Creek west of Hanson Meadows. However, this route misses the spectacular views of the upper three forks of Kelly Creek, Rhodes Peak and other vistas. Turn left on Trail #428 going up Hanson Ridge and Bruin Ridge to Fish Lake. It's at least nine miles from the Hanson Ridge junction to Fish Lake. Proceeding on, cruise north on the Bitterroot Divide toward a series of lakes on the Montana side, and the Steep Lakes and Goose Lake on the Idaho side. Goose Lake has well-established campsites, and it's a premium place to stop. The Centennial Trail continues on the stateline ridge past a bevy of lakes on the Montana side to Hoodoo Pass. Trails peel off to the high lakes in Montana, if you're so inclined.

Trail description for Centennial West (multiple use) to Hoodoo Pass: This section of Centennial West travels through a wide diversity of terrain, from big open ridges to wide lush meadows. It also travels through some old Burlington Northern property that was sold to Plum Creek Timber Co., which has logged many of the BN lands in the North Fork of the Clearwater country in the last decade or so. To begin, head north out of the Kelly Creek Guard Station for about two miles to the Pollock Ridge Trail #478. This trail is open to motorcycles, mountain bikes, hikers and pack stock. There are muddy spots, however, that will make for difficult passage. Please tread lightly. It's a long, arduous climb up Pollock Ridge, rising from 3,300 feet to Pollock Hill (5,503 feet) and a high point of 5,970 feet at a pass on the shoulder of Wapito Point. It's about nine miles from the Pollock Ridge trailhead to the pass. Once on the pass, you'll enjoy excellent views of a series of peaks along the Bitterroot (stateline) Divide and Fish Lake below. Ignore the high ridge trail at the pass and drop into the headwaters of Lake Creek, a choice spot for camping. The Centennial West route follows the entire length of Lake Creek (about nine miles) until it dumps into the North Fork of the Clearwater River. At the mouth of Lake Creek, you'll come to a lovely spot called The Cedars, a beautiful grove of old-growth western red cedar trees. The trail follows a dirt road by The Cedars. When the road crosses Long Creek, watch for a trailhead for Trail #373, a single-track trail that follows the North Fork of the Clearwater on the right bank. In about four miles, you'll come to a junction with Vanderbilt Gulch, where the trail splits. Follow the right fork, Trail #373, up the North Fork. Be ready for multiple creek crossings in this section. In about 3.5 miles, the trail abruptly leaves the North Fork and climbs 2,200 feet toward Hoodoo Pass. The trail will meet a 4WD jeep trail about a mile from the ridge separating Idaho and Montana. Here, you'll join up with the Stateline Trail and the main Centennial Trail route. Turn right and head about 1.5 miles to reach Hoodoo Pass. Turn left on the Stateline Trail if you wish to continue traveling north on the main Centennial Trail.

Historical and interpretive notes: Kelly Creek and several adjacent peaks were named after an early day prospector in the area.

Looking into Fish Lake from above. Fishing anyone?

Fish and critters: Fishing for native west-slope cutthroat in Kelly Creek is a special thrill for anglers. Please release your fish: Kelly Creek is a catch and release stream. The west-slope cutthroat trout is one of three endemic cold water fish species in Idaho. The two others are bull trout and rainbow trout. This cutthroat received its name because it can be found only on the west slope of the Continental Divide. On the trail there is a series of lakes that can be fished. One of the most popular is Fish Lake in Idaho with campground sites that can also be accessed by a six-mile, two-track trail from forest road 295... **A resident moose** lives at Goose Lake and can usually be observed feeding at dawn and dusk. Elk and deer can be seen anywhere along the trail, but especially in Hanson Meadows where they enjoy the summer habitat. In you're lucky, you may even see a black bear in this country. Less likely, but still possible, is your opportunity to hear a wolf calling. The Kelly Creek area is the site of one of the last verified Idaho sightings of a "natural" wolf. The large elk populations contribute to their presence.Also, if your timing is right, you can eat your way along some of the ridges working from one huckleberry patch to another. A feast for the eyes may be the single-stem white bear grass if you arrive at the right time.

#19 Hoodoo Pass to Mullan

South access: Hoodoo Pass, via Superior, Mont., or Kelly Creek
North access: Mullan, Idaho
Distance: About 66 miles
High point: 7,464 feet, near Eagle Cliff
Low point: 3,422 feet, South Fork Coeur d'Alene River, near Mullan
Type of trail: 2WD dirt road, single-track, 4WD dirt road
Uses allowed: Hiking and horseback; (in selected sections, mountain biking, motorcycles, and ATVs)
Terrain: Lush forest high-elevation terrain, rocky in places, overbrush, some blow-down.

Season: Late June to early October
Access to water: Spotty on high ridge; high lakes nearby
Overview map: Clearwater National Forest, Panhandle National Forests, St. Joe National Forest
Topo maps: Hoodoo Pass, Illinois Peak, Sherlock Peak, Torino Peak, Berge Peak, DeBorgia South, McGee Peak, Adair, Saltese, Mullan.

Directions to South Access: Drive to Hoodoo Pass via Superior, Mont., or the Kelly Creek Road #255 via Pierce. Superior, Mont., is on Interstate 90, about half way between Mullan, Idaho, and Missoula, Mont.

Directions to North Access: Drive to Mullan, Idaho. Mullan is located about 50 miles east of Coeur d'Alene, on Interstate 90. The Centennial Trail route drops into the town of Mullan on Willow Creek (the trail to Stevens Lake), across from Deadman Gulch.

Best resupply points: Kellogg, Wallace, Mullan or Superior, Mont., and Missoula, Mont.

Caution: Carry a water purifier for treating water.

Trail description: Get ready for a magnificent skyline ridge cruise on the Idaho-Montana divide, following the Stateline National Recreation Trail. As the ridge snakes to the north from Hoodoo Pass, you'll pass by many peaks and high mountain lakes along the Bitterroot Divide. The trail is very scenic, but in places, it can be hard to find or follow because of thick brush, rocks, downfall and lack of maintenance. Multiple-use trail users, including mountain bikers, motorcyclists and ATVs, can follow the portion of this Centennial Trail route from Dry Saddle to St. Paul Pass. The other portions on the Stateline Trail are single-track, so ATVs are

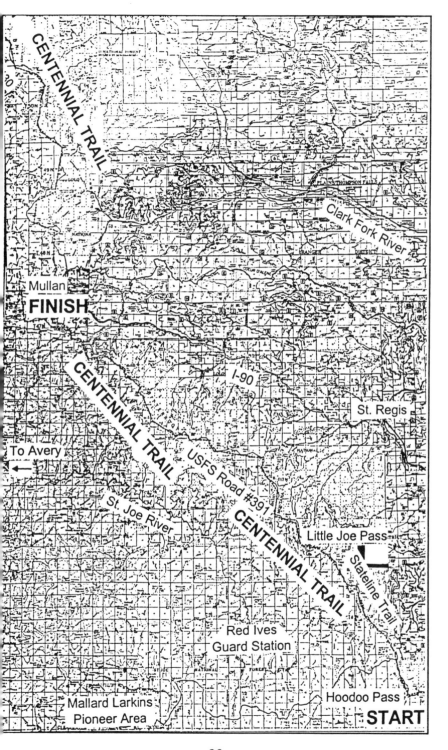

CENTENNIAL TRAIL

Clark Fork River

Mullan
FINISH

I-90

St. Regis

To Avery

CENTENNIAL TRAIL

USFS Road #391

St. Joe River

CENTENNIAL TRAIL

Little Joe Pass

Stateline Trail

Red Ives
Guard Station

Mallard Larkins
Pioneer Area

Hoodoo Pass

START

not allowed, and some of the single-track may be too technical for mountain bikers
To begin, pick up the main Centennial Trail route at Hoodoo Pass and head north
on a 4WD jeep trail for 1.5 miles to a junction with the Stateline Trail. The trail
tread turns to single-track and heads north. It's about 3.5 miles of uphill travel to
Graves Peak (7,360 feet). Just short of Graves Peak, the trail traverses the headwa-

Leo Hennessy

*Classic scene on the Idaho-Montana divide near Hoodoo
Pass in the Bitterroot Range.*

ters of the St. Joe
River, a national wild
and scenic river and a
favorite fishing
destination. Hikers
may want to camp in
this beautiful high
alpine basin. At this
point, you'll cross into
the St. Joe National
Forest, one of three
units of the Panhandle
National Forests. The
trail continues north
on the ridge spine to
the back shoulder of
Illinois Peak and then
it descends gradually
as it passes by Oregon
Lakes, Oregon Peak

and Missoula Lake, all on the Montana side of the divide.There is a road that leads
to a campsite above Missoula Lake, a good place to fill up with water. Above
Missoula Lake, you'll cross over a jeep trail and continue north, at an uphill cant. I
about two miles, another series of lakes will come into view on the Montana side –
first the Bonanza Lakes, two jewels sitting side by side, and then a series of tiny
lakes below aptly named Binocular Peak (7,260 feet). A pack trail drops into
Bonanza Lakes and Lost Lake, if you're inclined to visit them. Happily, the
Centennial Trail skirts Binocular Peak and holds elevation at about 6,800 feet as it
travels north toward a very steep-faced bowl that surrounds Heart Lake #1 and #2.
A trail drops into Heart Lake, if you're interested in camping there. Proceeding on,
the Stateline/Centennial Trail climbs to the high point of this section, a ridge point
just below Eagle Cliff (7,545 feet). You may want to take a moment to climb Eagle
Cliff for a nice view of Cliff Lake and Diamond Lake in the headwaters of Torino
Creek. There's a developed campground at Diamond Lake. You'll also see a dirt
road climbing up to the Stateline Trail from the Montana side. You will cross paths
with the dirt road about two miles from Eagle Cliff, at Dry Saddle. Here, you need
to pick up USFS Road #391, a jeep trail that will stay on the Idaho-Montana divide
all the way to Mullan. Follow #391 toward Little Joe Mountain and stay on the jeep
trail as it proceeds north. It will be obvious at this point that you've entered a major
logging zone on both the Idaho and Montana sides of the divide. Some of the

logging roads on the Idaho side come very close to USFS #391, but they should be avoided to stay on the ridgetop and keep your elevation. About four miles from Little Joe, you'll come to Black Peak (6,495 feet) and see Moore Lake off to the right. There is road access and a campground at Moore Lake. The town of St. Regis, Mont., will come into view, as will a paved road along the St. Joe River on the Idaho side. Stay on #391 and proceed north, now on a slightly downhill gradient, for about four miles to a four-way junction at Gold Summit (5,770 feet). USFS Road #431 comes in from the Montana side, and USFS #339 from the Idaho side. These are major log haul routes. Cross the logging roads and stay on #391, heading for Summit Springs. There is a spring here if you need to replenish water supplies. The next point of interest is Flattop Mountain (6,392 feet), a peak that looks as though it got a crewcut by nature.

Roger Williams

St. Joe Lake lies in a lovely basin on the Idaho side of the Bitterroot Divide.

Watch for a jeep road to split off to the right after Flattop. Stay left at this point on #391. The route remains mostly level in this section, while the trail passes just below the horizon line, depriving Centennial Trail travelers from seeing Square Lake, Hazel Lake, Mary Lake and Hub Lake just below Ward Peak. A pack trail splits off to access Ward Peak and the lakes, if you so desire. Continuing north on #391, the trail goes up and down past Clear Lake and Heart Lake before skirting the back shoulder of Craddock Peak (6,350 feet). It's more up and down, a yo-yo kind of experience, as you travel by Quarles Peak, Crittenden Peak and Dominion Peak. Just prior to Dominion Peak, old mining shafts and prospects indicate that you're entering an historic mining zone. Mullan is not too far now. Just past Bald Mountain, #391 heads for St. Paul Pass, under which the 1.8-mile Taft Tunnel crosses between Idaho and Montana. The jeep road ends at St. Paul Pass and a pack trail begins again on the stateline divide. It's about 2.5 miles to Bullion Pass, where a dirt road crosses the pack trail. Proceed on the trail another five miles to a point where the stateline ridge bends 90 degrees to the north, and you're overlooking Upper and Lower Stevens Lake (just past the St. Regis Lakes). The Centennial Trail route drops into the Stevens Lakes basin and follows a steep single-track trail about 2.5 miles down Willow Creek to the valley floor at the South Fork of the Coeur d'Alene River, just east of Mullan. The trail turns into a jeep road in lower Willow Creek at a three-way junction. Be sure to head straight down the draw in the middle of the three roads for the most direct route to the valley.

#20 Mullan to Clark Fork

South access: Mullan, 50 miles east of
Coeur d'Alene on I-90.
North access: Clark Fork, 30 miles east of
Sandpoint
Distance: About 75 miles
High point: Idaho Point, 6,505 feet
Low point: Clark Fork, 2,076 feet
Type of trail: 4WD dirt road, single-track
wilderness trail
Uses allowed: Hiking, equestrians, moun-
tain biking, motorcycles, ATVs, skiers and
snowmobiles
Terrain: Rolling and steep jeep trail and
single-track trail on Stateline Divide. Watch out for confusing logging road inter-
sections.
Season: Late June to late September
Access to water: Good to excellent; some open ridge sections have no water.
Watch for springs.
Overview map: Panhandle National Forests, Coeur d'Alene National Forest.
Topo maps: Derr Point, Cabinet, Jordan Creek, Gem Peak, Taylor Peak, Bloom
Peak, Murray, Black Peak, Thompson Pass, Lookout Pass.

Directions to South Access: Drive to Mullan, Idaho, about 50 miles east of Coeur
d'Alene on I-90. Pick up the Centennial Trail at the bottom of Deadman Gulch, just
east of Mullan, on the road to Shoshone Park Campground and Hale Fish Hatchery.
The Centennial Trail leaves the dirt road at Hale Fish Hatchery, the junction with
the Little North Fork of the South Fork Coeur d'Alene River.

Directions to North Access: Drive to Clark Fork, Idaho, via Idaho State Highway
200, about 30 miles east of Sandpoint.

Trail description: The Centennial Trail climbs out of Mullan at a fairly ambitious
clip to jump on the Stateline Divide, Cooper Pass (5,802 feet) and Glidden Pass
(5,766 feet) in just a few miles, but 2,200 feet above Mullan. Be sure to capitalize
on the potential side hikes and camping opportunities by high mountain lakes in the
first section of the trail, for there are fewer lakes in the second half. For the most
part, this segment follows some single-track trail and mostly 4WD jeep roads along
the rolling and steep Stateline Divide, varying from 5,000 to 6,500 feet in elevation.
Given that this section of the Centennial Trail is 75 miles long, eight or nine days
should be reserved for travel, depending on the mode of travel.

To begin, pick up the Centennial Trail at the bottom of Deadman Gulch, just east of

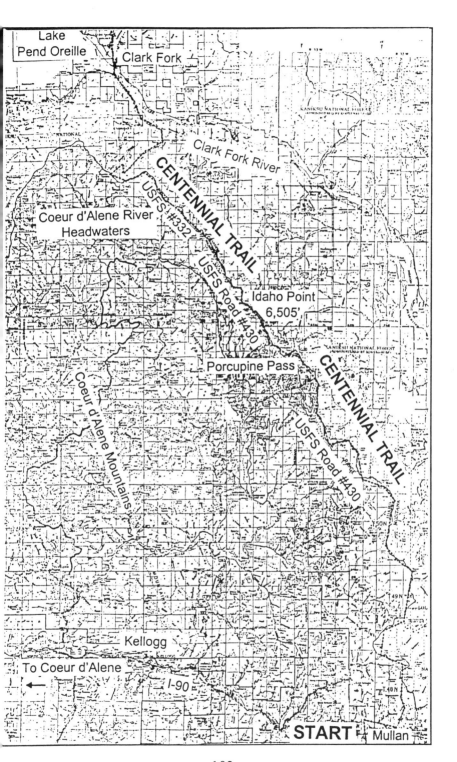

Lake Pend Oreille

Clark Fork

KANIKSU NATIONAL FOREST

Clark Fork River

CENTENNIAL TRAIL

USFS #332

USFS Road #430

Coeur d'Alene River Headwaters

Idaho Point 6,505'

KANIKSU NATIONAL FOREST

Porcupine Pass

CENTENNIAL TRAIL

USFS Road #430

Coeur d'Alene Mountains

Kellogg

To Coeur d'Alene

I-90

START — Mullan

103

Mullan, on the 2WD dirt road that goes to Shoshone Park Campground and Hale Fish Hatchery. You should be on the north side of the South Fork Coeur d'Alene River. Proceed up the road past Shoshone Park Campground to Hale Fish Hatchery. Look for USFS Road #133 heading north, up the Little North Fork of the South Fork CDA River. Take #133 up the Little North Fork. About 2.5 miles north of the fish hatchery, the 4WD road shrinks into a single-track trail at a Y-junction. Bear

Marty Morache

right and climb up a series of switchbacks toward Burke Summit (6,610 feet). The pack trail stays well below the summit and intersects two dirt roads just before Cooper Pass and a set of powerlines. Ignore the jeep road that heads east into Cooper Gulch. Proceed north on the dirt road, under the powerlines, to Cooper Pass. Bear right at another junction on the pass and continue on to Glidden Pass (5,766 feet). Upper Glidden

This section of the Centennial Trail is a trail-riders' dream because a series of roads snake along the Idaho-Montana divide most of the way.

Lake is accessible about one mile to the west of Cooper Pass or Glidden Pass, if you wish to camp there. There's more options just ahead, however. About one-half mile past Cooper Pass, turn right (north) on a 4WD jeep trail that goes to a three-way junction at Glidden Pass. Turn left on the pack trail heading in a northwesterly direction along the Stateline Divide. Now you're headed for several excellent camping opportunities at Park Lake, a tiny lake on the Montana side, and upper and lower Blossom Lakes, also on the Montana side. Proceeding on, the Centennial Trail heads for Thompson Pass, but stays well to the east of it. It's about two miles from Lower Blossom Lake to a point where the trail crosses a dirt road that heads for Thompson Pass. Continue on the trail, now #404, in a northerly direction on the Stateline Divide. It's about six miles to the next major junction. In three miles, you'll pass by a junction with a trail leading to Beaver Lakes and Beaver Peak. The side trip may be worthwhile to either on a nice day. About three miles northwest of the Beaver Peak trail, Trail #404 intersects USFS Road #430, a major road on the Stateline Divide that continues for the next two-thirds of this particular section. USFS Road #430 is well-marked most of the way. It's confusing in places at ridgetop junctions as to which road to follow. If in doubt, stay on the uppermost ridge. As you proceed north toward Black Peak, views to the left into Idaho provide a bird's-eye look at the North Fork of the Coeur d'Alene River, and the Shoshone

Mountain Range, which parallels the upper river canyon. There is a trail spur that heads to a USFS lookout at the summit of Black Peak. About three miles north of Black Peak, two high mountain lakes appear out of the forest green on the Montana side, East Lake and Berry Lake, both in the headwaters of Trout Creek. Remember, streams called Trout Creek often promise good fishing. You will see two junctions for the Trout Creek National Recreation Trail on the way to Bloom Peak. The Trout Creek trail offers a 19-mile motorcycle and mountain bike loop for those inclined. Just below Bloom Peak, there's a high lake on the Montana side called 93 Mile Lake. Worth taking a side trip, if you've got the time. On the Idaho side, from this area, it's possible to take a trail to the "Settlers Grove of Ancient Cedars," in the upper west fork of Eagle Creek.

Roger Williams

When the trail turns to single-track on the Bitterroot Divide, it's a gnarly up-and-down goat trail.

Proceeding on, the Centennial Trail continues on a northwest bead on the yo-yo like ridge 4WD jeep trail, #430. Logging roads get increasingly concentrated as you proceed north from Bloom and Lost Peak to 87 Mile Peak and Porcupine Pass. At the three-way junction at Porcupine Pass, proceed west on a 4WD road. It turns to a pack trail in about 200 yards or so from the pass. The pack trail parallels some logging roads that come and go, until you pass underneath the shadow of Idaho Point, and then it rejoins USFS Road #430 for about seven miles from Ulm Peak (6,444 feet) to Divide Peak (5,205 feet). By the time you get to Divide Peak, it's obvious that the ridgeline is beginning a long descent into Clark Fork. However, it's still a solid 15 miles of travel from Divide Peak to Clark Fork, now on USFS Road #332. For mountain bikes, motorcycles and ATVs, it'll be a raging descent. Hikers may want to stay one more night on the ridge. At the top of Dry Creek, it's possible to drop into Clark Fork via the major 2WD dirt road, or drop into town via a more primitive jeep trail, #277, in Twin Creek. At the junction at the bottom of the hill, turn left and follow the paved road into town alongside the railroad tracks. It's six-eight miles into town from here, depending on whether you dropped down via Twin Creek or Dry Creek. Enjoy the gravity-driven descent into this gorgeous, moist area on the east arm of Lake Pend Oreille -- a rewarding sight!

#21 Clark Fork to U.S. 95

South access: Clark Fork, Idaho
North access: USFS Road #404, just south
of Naples.
Distance: 51 miles
High point: Mount Pend Oreille, 6,755 feet
Low point: Clark Fork, 2,076 feet
Type of trail: Single-track forest trail, 4WD
dirt road
Uses allowed: Hiking, horseback; some
portions open to mountain bikes, motor-
cycles, ATVs and automobiles.
Terrain: Dense forest and rocky terrain;
thick overbrush and downfall likely. Watch
for washouts.
Season: Late June to early October
Access to water: Excellent.
Overview map: Panhandle National Forests, Kaniksu National Forest
Topo maps: Naples, Twentymile Creek, Clifty Mountain, Mt. Pend Oreille, Trestle
Peak, Clark Fork

Directions to South Access: Drive to Clark Fork, Idaho, on Idaho State Highway
200. Clark Fork is about 30 miles, east of Sandpoint. Because of unresolved access
problems on Trail #120, north of Clark Fork, drive up Lightning Creek Road #419
to Porcupine Lake Road #642 and head for Porcupine Lake Campground to tie into
the Centennial Trail. On USFS Road #419, you'll need to cross East Fork Creek in a
4WD vehicle. Continue another 2.5 miles to the Porcupine Lake Road #642 and
turn left. It's six miles to Porcupine Lake. Pick up Trail #114 at the campground
and climb three miles to the ridge and a junction with Trail #120. Turn right and
head up Trail #120. You're on the Centennial Trail.

Directions to North Access: Take U.S. 95/U.S. 2 north out of Sandpoint about 20
miles north to the signed turnoff for USFS Road #404, just south of Naples. Find a
place to park. The Centennial Trail heads up #404.

Best resupply points: Sandpoint or Bonners Ferry. In a pinch, Hope or Clark Fork.

Trail description: Get ready for some primo mountain-top hiking in the Cabinet
Mountains, north of Lake Pend Oreille. The Centennial Trail climbs from 2,085 feet
at Clark Fork and Lake Pend Oreille to a number of 6,000-foot peaks on the
Northern Idaho skyline, including Mount Pend Oreille, at 6,755 feet the high point
of the journey. This is North Idaho, folks, which means it rains a lot in the spring
and fall, so be sure to bring your rain gear. It's also grizzly country, so take precau-
tions, such as hanging your food away from camp. As you travel this section of the

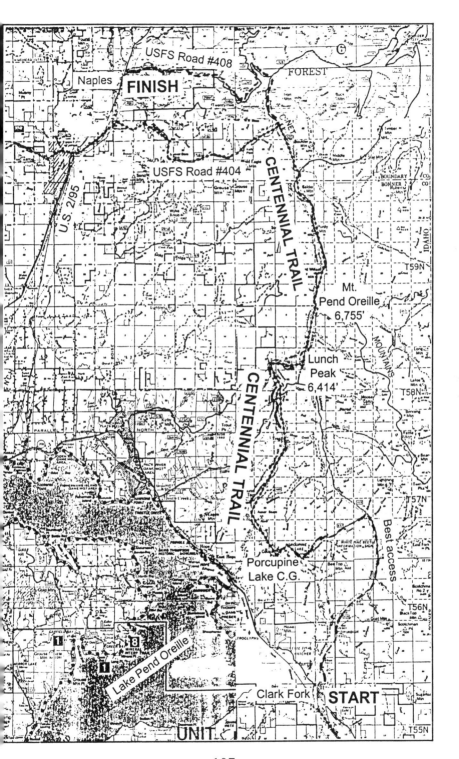

Centennial Trail, remember that you're in David Thompson country, an early British fur-trapper who was the first European to lay eyes on the Panhandle region. Thompson found the area so rich in furs and game that he built a trading post on the northeast corner of Land Pend Oreille. There is an historical monument to David Thompson in Hope. **To begin**, head north out of Clark Fork on the Lightning Creek Road #419 Because of unresolved access problems on Trail #120, you'll need to access the Centennial Trail via the Porcupine Lake Road #642 and Porcupine Lake Campground. Please be aware that you'll need to cross East Fork Creek in a 4WD vehicle about eight miles north of Clark Fork. Continue another 2.5 miles to the Porcupine Lake Road #642 and turn left. It's six miles to Porcupine Lake Campground. Pick

Mark Lisk

Centennial Trail travelers will enjoy big vistas of Lake Pend Oreille from the Cabinet Mountains, north of Clark Fork.

up Trail #114 at the campground and climb three miles to the ridge and a junction with Trail #120. Turn right and head north on Trail #120. Now, you're on the Centennial Trail. Trail #120 climbs to Cougar Peak (6,004 feet) and continues north to Round Top Mountain (6,149 feet). Ignore the junction with USFS Road #489 and follow Trail #120 on the ridge to Trestle Peak (6,032 feet). Trail #56 comes in from the right here to drop into Lightning Creek. Proceed north about three miles, where you'll come to USFS Road #275, which drops down Trestle Creek to Lake Pend Oreille. Go left on the road a short distance to a hairpin turn. Turn right and follow USFS Road #1091 up Smorgasbord Creek to a lookout at Lunch Peak (6,414 feet). Hook up with a single-track trail to the north of the peak, Trail #67, a well-maintained trail, and climb the ridge to Mount Pend Oreille (6,755 feet), about three miles away. Just prior to Mount Pend Oreille, it's possible to take a side trip on Trail #52 to Lake Darling, a possible campsite with water about 2.5 miles away. Otherwise, continue north from Mount Pend Oreille to Purdy Mountain (6,062 feet) and Calder Mountain (5,699 feet). As you pass by Mount Willard, watch for a seep of water right on the trail, a rare source of water on the high ridge. Just before Calder Mountain, Trail #488 comes in from the left and heads down to Grouse Creek and USFS Road #280, a well-traveled access road that ends up at U.S. 95. This is a possible bail-out area, if you need to end your trip early.

Proceeding on, about 1.5 miles north of Calder Mountain, the Centennial Trail peels off to the left on USFS Road #427, a 4WD jeep trail that descends into Boulder Creek. The official Centennial Trail route follows #427 for about three miles to a junction with Rummy Creek trail, a poorly maintained trail, the Forest Service reports. The Rummy Creek trail to Kelly Pass is choked with overbrush and downfall, and difficult, if not impossible to find, Forest Service officials say. Call ahead to the Bonners Ferry Ranger District for the latest conditions. The most dependable route out of the Cabinets and down to U.S. 95 is to stay on #427 another four miles to USFS #408, a major access road that descends to U.S. 95 over about 12 miles.

It's possible to return to the north access point, USFS Road #404, by following #408 to Twentymile Pass, and then go left on USFS Road #2686 and follow it about seven miles downhill to #404. This alternative takes you on a tour of Twentymile Peak, and it is a well-used road, according to the Forest Service.

Historical and interpretive notes: When you're standing on top of **Mount Pend Oreille**, the views of Lake Pend Oreille, one of the largest freshwater lakes west of the Mississippi River, should be spectacular. The lake, which was carved by glacial activity, is very deep, about 1,150 feet at its deepest point. The lake also has 111 miles of shoreline, stretching from Bayview on the south to Sandpoint and Clark Fork to the north ... **British fur trapper David Thompson** was the first-known white man to set foot in the Kootenai Valley in the spring of 1808. He came there in search of furs for the North West Co. He established a fur trading post, called the Kullyspell House in September 1809, to begin a long relationship of trading with the Kalispel, Flathead, Spokan and Coeur d'Alene Indians. Thompson later settled in Montreal, where he died at the age of 87. A monument to Thompson is located in the town of Hope ... **The Clark Fork River** runs for 420 miles -- mostly in western Montana -- before it flows into Lake Pend Oreille as the lake's primary source of water ... The **Clark Fork** is named for William Clark from the Lewis and Clark expedition, and so is the town, since it was named for the river ... French trappers named the **Cabinet Mountains** after the cabinet-like recesses in the sheer walls of the mountains.

#22 U.S. 95 to Indian Creek C.G.

South access: Junction of U.S. 95 and
County Road 47, Pack River Road
North access: Indian Creek Campground,
Priest Lake
Distance: About 30 miles
High point: Selkirk Mountain pass, 6,400
feet
Low point: U.S. 95, 2,140 feet
Type of trail: Single-track forest trail, 2WD
road, 4WD dirt road
Uses allowed: Hiking, horseback; some
portions open to mountain bikes, motor-
cycles, ATVs and automobiles.

Terrain: Dense forest and rocky terrain,
thick overbrush and downfall likely. Watch for washouts.
Season: Late June to early October
Access to water: Excellent
Overview map: Panhandle National Forests, Kaniksu National Forest
Topo maps: Priest Lake SE, Mount Roothaan, Dodge Peak, Naples

Directions to South Access: Take U.S. 95/U.S. 2 north out of Sandpoint about 12
miles north to the signed turnoff for Pack River Road (County Road 47 and USFS
Road #231). Turn left on the 2WD road and proceed up the Pack River Road about
13 miles to the Fault Lakes trailhead (Trail #59). Pick up the Centennial Trail here.

Directions to North Access: Head north on State Highway 57 from Priest River
about 15 miles to a junction with the Eastshore Drive of Priest Lake and the tiny
town of Coolin. Turn right and proceed along the east shore of Priest Lake, past
Cavanaugh Bay, to Indian Creek Campground.

Best resupply points: Sandpoint or Priest River. In a pinch, Coolin or Nordman.

Trail description: This section of the Centennial Trail has a number of unresolved
public access problems on private lands to the west of McArthur Wildlife Management Area, so we recommend taking the Pack River Road to the McCormick Creek
Trail and bypass the problem spots for now. We hope the Bonners Ferry Ranger
District and private landowners can work out the access problems in the future so
the public can gain access to points west of McArthur WMA. Once on public land,
however, this route features some beautiful areas as you cross over the Selkirk
Mountains near Hunt Peak and Gunsight Peak and enjoy high vistas of Priest Lake
before dropping down to Indian Creek State Park. Please note that the Centennial
Trail route along Hunt Creek, on the west slope of the Priest Lake State Forest, is
open to all forms of multiple-use because it's a 4WD road. But when you enter the

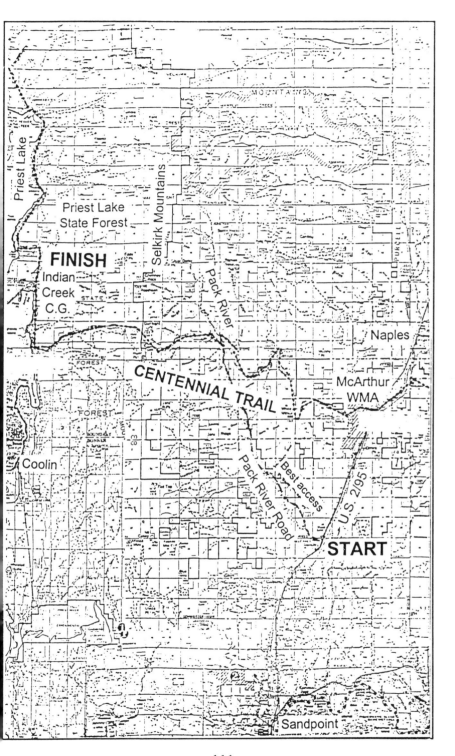

Priest Lake

Priest Lake
State Forest

FINISH

Indian
Creek
C.G.

Selkirk Mountains

Pack River

MOUNTAINS

PURCELL

Naples

CENTENNIAL TRAIL

McArthur
WMA

FOREST

Coolin

Pack River Road

Best access

U.S. 2/95

START

Sandpoint

111

Selkirk Mountain Primitive Area, only hiking and stock use are allowed.

To begin, head west on the Fault Lake Trail #59 for the Fault Lakes basin. It's a fairly steep climb over about 6.5 miles, with several switchbacks into the lakes basin. This would be a good place to camp. Consider side-hiking along the Selkirk Crest after you get to the lakes. Gunsight Peak (7,352 feet) is nearby, and farther north, there is Mount Roothan (6,842 feet) and Chimney Rock, both signature features of the Selkirk Mountain range. There is no trail to the north, however, so hikers will have to bushwhack on the serrated rocky ridge.

From the upper lake on the north side of the Fault Lakes basin, climb over the top of the Selkirk Crest (this is a bushwhack scramble; there is no trail over the top) and drop into Hunt Lake, a large and beautiful alpine lake on the west slope. When you reach Hunt Lake, pick up the single-track trail on the west end of the lake and head down Hunt Creek. The single-track trail forks in about a mile at a junction with the Hunt Peak trail. Stay to the right unless you want to side hike to Hunt Peak. Soon after that junction, there will be another fork when the single-track trail meets a 4WD road that winds into the South Fork of Hunt Creek. Stay to the right on the single-track trail, which ends in a mile and turns into a 4WD road. Follow the road down Hunt Creek and enjoy a long descent (about 5.5 miles) into the east side of Priest Lake. Multiple use is allowed on this section of the trail. Follow your map closely as you descend, because a number of logging roads will create confusion. If you end up on a logging road that bends away from Hunt Creek, you went the wrong direction. The Hunt Creek access road stays along Hunt Creek the whole way down, except for a number of switchbacks about two miles above Priest Lake.

At the junction of Hunt Creek Road and the East Shoreline road of Priest Lake, turn right on the paved two-lane road and proceed about three miles to Indian Creek State Park, the end of this section of the Centennial Trail.

To extend your trip in this area by about 10 miles, one could tie into the Martin Creek Trail #222 off the Pack River Road, and head up to Dodge Peak, which is part of the original Centennial Trail route in this area. There are no access problems from Martin Creek to Dodge Peak. The Martin Creek Trail dissolves into a 4WD road about four miles up the drainage. Then, the jeep road heads for Dodge Peak (5,027 feet). From here, take USFS Road #2605 to the west for about five miles to the Pack River Road. At this junction, head south for a quarter-mile and pick up the Centennial Trail route, Trail #59, heading for Fault Lake.

Another side-trip option from Dodge Peak is to travel south about four miles on Trail #453, a primitive two-track, along a high ridge to White Mountain (5,005 feet). This is all national forest land in between the two peaks, which offer nice views of Lake Pend Oreille. It's also part of the original Centennial Trail route. It's an out-and-back affair, however, because there are access problems between White Mountain and McArthur WMA.

It's a sobering thought to realize that as you venture into the Selkirks, you're entering "grizzly country." The Forest Service recommends hanging your food and leashing your dogs in the area.

Historical and interpretive notes: The **McArthur Wildlife Management Area** is an important nesting area for waterfowl. In fact, it was the first habitat area purchased by Idaho Fish and Game for waterfowl production. More than 400 geese hatched at McArthur WMA in 1989. Some 150 nesting structures and 30 artificial islands help increase duck and geese populations. Also, watch for coyotes, moose, and white-tailed deer in the area. Rest rooms and boat launching are available here ... **Ruby Ridge**, the place where white separatist Randy Weaver, his slain wife, Vicky, and their family had a bloody confrontation with the FBI in the early 1990s, is just north of McArthur Lake WMA. The case captured national headlines for months leading up the trial and eventual acquittal of Weaver. The Iowa man ended up winning a $3 million civil suit against the U.S. government ... **The Selkirk Mountains** stretch for miles to the north into British Columbia and Canada. The range forms one side of the Purcell Trench, a wide valley cleared by glaciers several hundred thousand years ago. The Selkirks are part of the Kaniksu Batholith, a granite formation.

#23-Indian Cr. C.G. to Canadian border

South access: Indian Creek Campground, east side of Priest Lake
North access: Forest Road #1013, Canadian border
Distance: 37 miles
High point: 4,100 feet Upper Priest Falls
Low point: 2,900 feet
Type of trail: Single-track, jeep trail, paved road
Uses allowed: Hiking, equestrians, mountain bikes; portions open to ATVs and motorcycles
Terrain: Rolling, rocky in places, boggy spots
Season: Early May to early October
Access to water: Plentiful
Overview map: Panhandle National Forest (Kaniksu portion)
Topo maps: Priest River, Chimney Rock, Sandpoint, Lake Pend Oreille

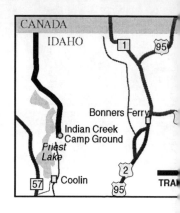

Southern access: Head north on State Highway 57 from Priest River about 15 miles to a junction with the Eastshore Drive of Priest Lake to the tiny town of Coolin. Turn right and proceed along the east shore of Priest Lake, past Cavanaugh Bay, to Indian Creek Campground. This portion of the Centennial Trail runs parallel to Priest Lake and Upper Priest Lake.

Northern access: Head north on State Highway 57 from the town of Priest River and proceed 35 miles along the west side of Priest Lake, past Nordman, to Forest Road #302. This is a well-maintained paved road that turns to dirt north of Nordman. Continue past Granite Falls, and turn right at Granite Pass on Forest Road #1013. Proceed for 12 miles to the northern-most trailhead of the Centennial Trail. The trailhead is marked as the Priest River Trail, about 10 miles south of the Canadian border. This trail is open to non-motorized use: hiking, stock use and mountain biking.

Trail description: The northern-most section of the Idaho Centennial Trail is, without a doubt, one of the most scenic segments of trail anywhere in Idaho. The route begins with a scenic cruise along the east shoreline of Priest Lake on a mixture of primitive roads and trails, and then north of Upper Priest Lake, it follows well-maintained single-track tread along upper Priest River and winds through dense old-growth cedar forest and grizzly bear habitat. Tall ferns and second-growth trees fill in the shady forest under the giant canopy of 500-year-old cedar trees. Folks will hear the trickle of the Priest River as they enjoy the trail. **To begin,** follow Eastshore Road along the east shore of Priest Lake for about 12 miles to Lionhead State Park, on the northeast corner of Priest Lake. Proceed past the park's northern boundary about 200 yards. Then, on your left, watch for a large berm at a

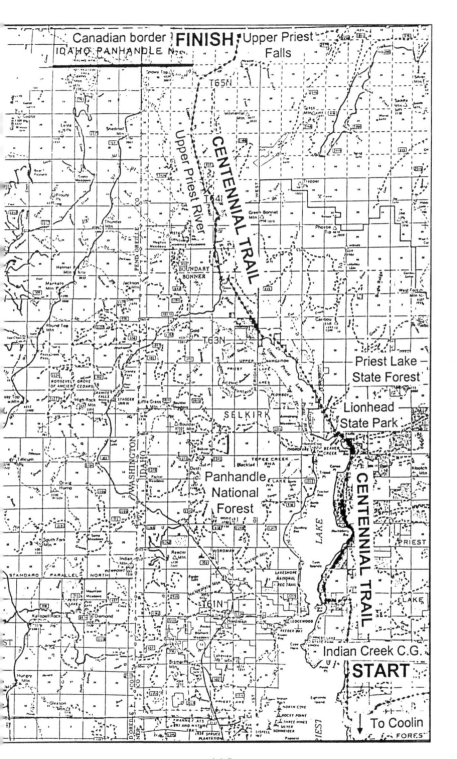

Roger Williams

The Upper Priest River trail is well-shaded by moss-covered old-growth cedar trees. Volunteers built a number of wooden bridges to cross bogs and creeks.

junction with a primitive two-track trail heading into the woods. Go left and follow the two-track. The trail crosses Caribou Creek in about a mile. Ford the creek and continue on the two-track through the wet, dense forest. Soon, Upper Priest Lake will come into view. The two-track will head downhill and dissolve into a single-track trail and continue along the east side of Upper Priest Lake. In about three miles, you'll come to a junction with the Trapper Creek Trail. There is a nice primitive campsite at Trapper Creek, if you wish to camp there. There is also a side hike possible on Trapper Creek.

Continuing on, the single-track leaves Upper Priest Lake and follows the east side of Upper Priest River, now Trail #302, for about four miles to a junction with a logging road and the trailhead for Trail #302. Turn left on the dirt road and follow it to a T-intersection with USFS Road #1013, a major dirt access road. Turn right and follow #1013 for about six miles to the north. After traveling six miles, watch for a well-marked trailhead and parking area on the left for the Upper Priest River Trail, #308. The Centennial Trail route follows the beautiful Upper Priest River Trail, a well-maintained single-track, for 10 miles to Upper Priest Falls. The trail ends at the falls, so people will not actually be able to reach the Canadian border without a gnarly bushwhack through thick brush and timber. A number of wooden bridges on the trail provide good crossings across many boggy areas and small creek crossings. About eight miles toward Priest Falls, a junction appears on the right. Stay left to proceed to the falls, where a small pool waits for a refreshing swim on a hot summer day. **Mountain bikers can do a loop ride** on the Upper Priest Trail by dropping a vehicle at the Upper Priest River Trailhead and then continuing north in a series of logging roads to a point where a single-track trail peels off the road by Malcom Creek and connects to the Upper Priest Trail, south of the falls. Then, take the trail south back to the parking area. Be forewarned that the single-track trail dropping into Malcom Creek is steep and features a number of switchbacks. It is about a 20-mile loop, for strong riders only.

Leo Hennessy

Three members of the Grizzly Ridge Riders take a moment to rest on the north end of Upper Priest Lake.

Historical and interpretive notes: In this segment of the Centennial Trail, **the route passes through national forest and state Endowment Land.** Although most of the shoreline areas along Upper Priest Lake and Priest Lake have not been logged recently, most of the state lands to the east of the trail are commercial forest. We mention this to forewarn folks that log truck traffic is heavy along most dirt roads in this region, especially on the Caribou Hill Road (Forest Road #655)... **Priest Lake and the surrounding countryside** were formed by glaciation. Massive ice sheets pushed into the Panhandle region from Canada over 100,000 years ago. The polishing effect of glaciers gave the Priest Lake area the soft, sculpted look that it has today... **Priest Lake was named for Father John Roothaan,** an early missionary who visited the area in the early 1800s. At one time the lake was called Lake Roothaan, but its name was later changed when the Great Northern Railroad laid a new line through the Panhandle in the 1890s... **Priest Lake also has a long history of tourism.** A smattering of artists and movie stars, going back to the days when Nell Shipman films were shot on the shores of Priest Lake in the 1920s, have lived in the area for most of this century. Summertime in the Sandpoint area can never be complete without the annual music and art festivals...

Your comments, please

We'd like to know about your trip on any section on the Idaho Centennial Trail. People who actually visit the trail at the ground level have the best information about trail conditions, blowdown, trail washouts and other important things that you saw along the way.

Please take a moment to jot down your thoughts on the pages provided here, send us a letter, or send an e-mail to Leo Hennessy, state trails coordinator for the Idaho Department of Parks and Recreation. We plan to post the latest conditions about the Idaho State Centennial Trail on the web page of Idaho Parks and Recreation, when a new web site is finished in 1998.

Send your comments to Leo by e-mail at Lhenness@idpr.state.id.us, or send them in writing to Leo Hennessy, Idaho Department of Parks and Recreation, 5657 Warm Springs Ave., Boise, ID 83712. Phone: 208-334-4199.

Thank you.

Notes

Notes

Notes

Notes

Notes

Notes

Notes

Notes

Parting shot

Roger Williams

We think Syd Tate's hat says it all. Please come back again soon.